DRAW[N]

· FIRE · BRIGADE · STATION ·

Chiltern
FIREHOUSE

CHILTERN FIREHOUSE

THE COOKBOOK

NUNO MENDES   ANDRÉ BALAZS

PHOTOGRAPHY BY PEDEN & MUNK

TEN SPEED PRESS

California | New York

CONTENTS

THE FIRE BRIGADE

Stephen Fry

ONCE THERE WAS A LONDON with no Chiltern Firehouse and suddenly there was a London with one.

We should call to mind how absurd a proposition this establishment always was. With the deepest respect to the Portman and Howard de Walden Estates (who appear to own most of it), what exactly is Marylebone? An untidy polygon north of Oxford Street, uncomfortably sandwiched between Paddington and Fitzrovia. It is not Soho, St. James's, Covent Garden, or Mayfair. Not Knightsbridge, Belgravia, Kensington, or Chelsea. Chiltern Street itself is a huffing and puffing walk from any of those more fashionable districts, with their starred restaurants, glossy member clubs, glamorous watering holes, and illustrious and historic hotels.

I suppose I might have walked past the Manchester Square Fire Station, as it was once known, in my walks around town, but I am embarrassed to say I have no memory of ever doing so. When I heard that André Balazs, the owner of New York's Mercer Hotel and Hollywood's Chateau Marmont (before whose name it is almost obligatory to place the word "legendary") planned to convert this large derelict building, one of London's very first purpose-built firehouses, into a restaurant with twenty-six hotel suites, I murmured a silent secular prayer for him and thought little more of it. Bless. I mean, *Marylebone*? And not even bustling Marylebone High Street, but some lost thoroughfare in the anonymous hinterland east of Baker Street.

In the London hospitality trade, as in the world of West End theatre, people sometimes talk about "walk-past." That restaurant failed because it was in an area of London that diners don't visit. This show bombed because the theatre was off the beaten track. No walk-past means no walk-in, no spreading of the word, no reputation, no buzz, no business. In both fields of endeavor these mantras may seem a credible excuse in the event of failure, but actually they never are. Before I sent up my silent secular prayer I should have called to mind the *Field of Dreams* principle. If you build it, they will come. Which is to say, if you build it *right* they will come. No matter where it is.

Aside from the walk-past excuse, people like to imagine variables such as "luck" and "timing." That venture succeeded because it caught a quick wave of the moment. This one failed because the weather was awful for its first month. Or the opening clashed with the London Olympics. Or it didn't.

When the Chiltern Firehouse became—within a day of its opening—the most talked-about restaurant in London for a decade or more, there were plenty quick to attribute it to Balazs's address book, plump as it is with the names of so much paparazzo bait, so many movers and shakers—film actors, sporting heroes, and heavyweights of music and the media. The A-list early diners, so the narrative goes, created a momentum, a full reservations diary, and an instant reputation that generated the perfect storm of success. This being Britain, those who were ultra-cool in their own estimation couldn't wait to get a reservation and then claim loudly that they didn't see what the fuss was all about. Well, we can forget all that. Forget the paparazzi outside, forget the stories of ambassadors, prime ministers, and Oscar winners who couldn't get a table, forget the prattle about beautiful people, ugly behavior, and the whole Dolce Vita comes to London nonsense. The truth of the restaurant is that all are welcome, a table is so much easier obtained than the media storm would have you believe, and all who do come are treated with the same courtesy and hospitality.

The answer to the success of the Chiltern Firehouse is so much more interesting, so much more instructive, so much more beautiful than a story of celebrities and PR puff. And the answer is in your hands now.

Even a quick reading of the text and a thoughtful interpretation of what the photographs signify will reveal the truth. You will see that there are very few (*if any*) places in London where greater thought, expertise, effort, time, perfectionism, and originality have been put into the preparation of ingredients. Head Chef Nuno Mendes and his staff, backstage and front of house, teach in this book that no part of the Chiltern Firehouse story is to do with luck, timing, or film actors.

The cocktails alone: these are not quick and easy retreads familiar to anyone who has lived through the rise of metropolitan mixology and diplomas in "international bartending"; these are assemblies of

exquisite ingredients that owe everything to a deep understanding of how ice, alcohol, and essences interact. I have enjoyed so many cocktails here without ever knowing quite why they were so much better than any I had tried anywhere else. Ever. They make their best-in-the-world Manhattan using sous vide. Sous vide for heaven's sake! I mean, who knew? They have weekly staff syrup and maceration days, which explains how they can make cocktails that hum with fruit without shouting of sugar. But, as you will see, all this is more connected to old-fashioned jam- and jelly-making than to the cold laboratories of the molecular cuisine movement.

The food. Everyone knows that Americans will look at the most tempting, elaborate, and ambitious menus and after a brief inspection say to the waiter, "I'll have the Caesar salad." And so the Chiltern Firehouse does indeed offer a Caesar, but it's the best I have ever tasted. Inexplicably so, I might have said until I read Nuno's recipe.

Yes, this is first and foremost a recipe book.

If you are anything like me, the more you read, the more you will become convinced of the extraordinary passion and creativity with which everyone at the Firehouse approaches their work, and the more you will want to make tentative steps toward creating some of the great dishes here yourself.

I am writing this foreword because, of course, I love the restaurant. Everything about it. I love the stunning design, the incredibly convivial atmosphere, the dedicated and sweet-natured people who work there, and most of all I love what they do to food. So let me tell you what I will be trying to put together for myself in my kitchen. Let me offer you my menu.

I shall start with a Firehouse Sazerac (page 54), a classic New Orleans cocktail, endowed with a wicked kick of absinthe. I am nervous but excited about the Nut Syrup (page 54) it all depends upon. Yet imagine the feeling of triumph if I succeed.

The snacks that can come to your table while you read the menu are so preposterously delicious that is easy to overdo things and leave little room for much else. The American soul food bliss of the Bacon Cornbread Fingers with Chipotle Maple Butter (page 86) and the Fried Chicken with Smoky Bacon Ranch Dip (page 90) send me to heaven, so I shall certainly try and recreate them in my own kitchen. They are the dishes I shall order as my last on death row, in case you need to know.

The peerless Romain Audrerie can help me decide what to drink— he's the friendliest sommelier in London, and—for a Frenchman— wonderfully wise about world wines.

Red Mullet, Endive Hearts, Mussels, and Marcona Almonds (page 214). This is one of the best fish dishes I have tasted, and it seems simple. I shall certainly have a try at home.

If you read here about the lengths they go to to produce the perfect steak in the Firehouse, you will see why I won't be trying one of those recipes. I think I'd set off too many alarms—and I can't be too sure of getting a response from a fire crew since there's a shortage of fire stations in my area. Apparently everyone's rushing to convert them into restaurants. Stupid idea. So the main course I will try to recreate is the Spring Lamb (page 225); it genuinely looks doable even for a duffer like me.

The Frozen Apple Panna Cotta (page 260, which I call Snail in the Grass) is probably the best pudding ever constructed in the history of the world and if I could make that I would die happy.

Well, as you see, that's one of thousands of permutations that this book offers up. You will be able to create your own menus. Of course the food is serious and of a uniquely high caliber, seamlessly mixing comfort food with cuisine for grand lunches or dinners, but the lack of shortcuts and the fact that the emphasis is on patience and ingredients should not put us off. Far from it—it reminds us that this is how life works, and should work. It is a wonderful magic secret to success to discover that there are no wonderful magical secrets to success.

Only hard work, passion, patience, commitment, and—yes, I dare say it—love.

COCKTAILS

THE LOVE OF A GOOD COCKTAIL

EVERYONE ENGAGED IN A LOVE AFFAIR with cocktails knows, for certain, that their go-to drink is the climactic test of a bartender's skills. For Luis Simoes, who directs the bar menus at the Firehouse, that drink would be a Manhattan. Its components—whiskey, vermouth, bitters, and ice—represent the canonical ingredients upon which cocktail-making is formed.

HEY BARTENDER

No one knows exactly when the first ritual act of shaking or stirring those ingredients together took place. It may have been in New Orleans in the 1850s, or in New York a decade later: the invention of the cocktail is a tale as vague and convoluted as the birth of the blues. What is known, or at least strongly suspected, is that distilled spirits of that era had a rotgut charm that only a gunslinger in a Wild West saloon could appreciate neat. So spirits were already being mixed with other ingredients: the punches beloved of Charles Dickens and Enlightenment thinkers were an early prototype of the mixed cocktail, albeit without the vermouth.

Vermouths may (or may not) have been around since the time of the pharaohs. Their screwball history includes stints as curatives, royal elixirs, and an unlikely remedy for the plague. When they were first imported to America in the mid-nineteenth century, they found unexplained popularity among California's gold prospectors, earning the reputation as the drink of miners and whores. On the East Coast, meanwhile, they began to appear on higher-toned drinks lists, first as wines and then as mixers with spirits, often alongside splashes of aromatic bitters, which had begun to wend their way north from New Orleans.

How these ingredients met is ultimately less significant than the results of their consummation. Luis describes it as "a marriage in multiple dimensions," which is to say that creating the perfect cocktail is a ceaseless quest for harmony, with the constant possibility of discord. The bedrock is the spirit, but the varying profiles of spirits make it a fluid foundation. In Luis' words:

> In a Manhattan, using a single malt rather an American whiskey requires an entirely different vermouth. The vermouth counterbalances and answers the flavors in the whiskey. It is the bridge that connects all the ingredients. You want one unified flavor. It should evolve on the palate, but at no point should the whiskey, the vermouth, or the bitters dominate.

Creating the perfect cocktail is a ceaseless quest for harmony, with the constant possibility of discord.

Growing up, Luis went through the usual late-adolescent abuse of vermouth—his weakness was a Martini Rosso and Coke—but something clicked, and he left the sinner's tent with an appreciation for the complexities of the historic vermouths of Italy and France: "It changed my perception of drinks. The richness of vermouths—the amaros, rossos, biancos, rosés, each with their different combinations of floral notes, spices, vegetable notes, sweetness, and bitterness... they led me to think about cocktails differently, looking closer at their origin." There are more than fifty vermouths stocked at the Firehouse, and they play a crucial role in almost all our cocktails, and are often used in combinations of two or more varieties. An assortment of bitters—Angostura, orange, vanilla, grapefruit, Creole, chocolate, and hellfire—along with concentrates of lime, lemon, and orange serve to intensify flavor and add unsugared aromatics. Our house-made syrups and macerations (pages 42 to 65) are a professional bartender's way of capturing the essence of seasonal fruits and nuts without the sweetness and artificiality of flavored liqueurs. All that stands between these ingredients and a perfect cocktail is a short list of easily mastered rules and techniques that typically divide the pro and the amateur mixologist.

THE FIREHOUSE METHOD

THE ALCOHOL

Freshness is key. Don't imagine that the bottle of gin or whiskey that was opened a year ago will impart the depths of flavor that your cocktail craves. Spirits deteriorate like all alcohols, just more slowly. As a general rule, it's best to finish an opened bottle within six months. Gins and vodkas store well in the fridge, which will extend their life closer to a year. Vodka can be stored in the freezer, but gin not so much.

Vermouths decline much more rapidly. Always store them in the fridge once opened, and use up an opened bottle within three weeks. Vermouths are at their very best in the first week of being open.

THE ICE

Ice for cocktails should be made from filtered or distilled water and used smoking cold, straight from the freezer. Ice has two roles in drinks: to dilute and to chill. Of the two, diluting is unquestionably the more important. The ability to correctly dilute a drink is what makes for truly excellent cocktails, in the same way that proper seasoning elevates the simplest of dishes. Proper dilution allows a cocktail's often very intense ingredients to be tamed and blended together in harmony. The reduction in temperature is a happy coincidence of dilution. A cocktail must be properly diluted first, and at the correct temperature second. The reason for this is that a cocktail's temperature will change no matter what, but dilution is final (unless the drink is served on ice). Generally speaking, there is a direct correlation between chilling and melting, so a cocktail that is shaken or stirred to the perfect level of dilution will also be nice and cold. For a drink served on the rocks, always discard the mixing ice and add fresh ice to the serving glass. The purpose of the second ice is purely to maintain temperature without further diluting the

A fifty-pound block of ice, frozen slowly from distilled water. Hewn with a Japanese ice saw. Sculpted with a meat cleaver and mallet. Shaped into custom sizes for individual cocktails.

drink. Thus, for a drink such as an Old Fashioned, one giant cube, spherical or square, is optimal. Molds for making monster ice cubes are readily available, and are worth the small investment. Should you find yourself without one, a useful trick is to half-fill a rocks glass with filtered water and freeze it, then build the drink on top of the ice. In a short time, the sides of the glass will have warmed sufficiently to release a large, slow-melting cube that will last for half an hour or more.

STIRRING

A long-handled cocktail spoon is the essential stirring tool. The technique of stirring should be circular but gentle, so as not to smash the ice cubes. The purpose of stirring is to chill and dilute the drink, but also to change its density. As alcohol gets colder, it becomes more viscous, which gives a drink the heaviness that is the desired texture of a martini or Manhattan. The skill comes in knowing when you have hit the perfect apex of temperature, dilution, and density, after which the drink will start to become thin and watery. It's always better to stop on the early side if you're unsure. Your ally here will be the prechilled glass that you put in the freezer for a good half hour before serving.

A useful trick is to half-fill a rocks glass with filtered water and freeze it, then build the drink on top of the ice.

SHAKING

Moving the shaker up and down in jackhammer movements, as though trying to get ketchup out of the bottom of the bottle, is good for theatrics but not for your drink, because it will smash the ice cubes and create unwanted dilution. Instead, go for an elliptical, figure-eight motion. This allows the cocktail to wash over the ice cubes, forming bubbles of oxygen, which lead to a light texture in the finished cocktail.

THE TWIST

The piece of lemon or orange peel that a bartender twists over a drink before serving may look like showmanship, but the citrus oils that are released provide a final infusion of flavor, as well as an aroma that is the first note that registers when the drink is lifted toward the mouth. The piece of peel should be about 2 inches long, and cut thinly enough that the pith is barely visible. Typically, the peel is added to the drink as a garnish after the twist.

CONSIGLIERE AND MIXOLOGIST

The Firehouse has its own personality shaped by the utilitarian nature of the building and its history. It's simple and honest—exactly what we wanted the cocktail menu to be. We wanted everything on our cocktail menus to say "Chiltern Firehouse" and nowhere else. We wanted the Firehouse to feel like the best big house you've ever visited.

A good cocktail is a combination of the mood of the client, the sensibility of the barman, and the place it's served in. A good bartender should understand body language: Does this person want to be left alone? Does he want to talk? If it's a group, what's the dynamic? Who is the leader? Who is hanging back a little? Then it's about the mood: Have they had a hard day and need a pick-me-up? Are they embarking on a celebratory evening and want something that kicks things off? A good bartender is a combination of consigliere and mixologist. You can learn how to make cocktails; you can study flavor and spirit combinations. But that's not enough; you have to have a certain sparkle.

There are two bars at the Firehouse. The restaurant bar I always think of as a Victorian saloon bar, a place where a fireman would come and have a drink: simple and honest, you sit at the counter, really informal. The main bar is the chancel. Here it is about comfort and quiet ease. Making something seem homely and casual is very difficult, but that's what we want to achieve.

We know all the classic ways of making cocktails at the Firehouse: you won't find a better Manhattan or Old Fashioned in the world. But for me it's all about experimenting, pushing the boundaries, all with the final aim of achieving quality and harmony inside the glass.

MANHATTAN

SIMPLE METHOD

INGREDIENTS

Serves 1

2 ounces/60 ml bourbon
1½ ounces/40 ml Noilly Prat Rouge vermouth
1 dash Angostura bitters
1 dash orange citrate
1 strip unwaxed orange peel

Pour all the ingredients except the orange peel into a mixing glass filled with ice cubes, stir 25 times with a bar spoon, then strain and pour over fresh ice in a rocks glass. Garnish with the orange peel.

PRO METHOD

INGREDIENTS

Serves 8

15 ounces/450 ml bourbon
12 ounces/350 ml Noilly Prat Rouge vermouth
3½ ounces/100 ml Cherry Maceration (page 62)

3½ ounces/100 ml still water
8 dashes Angostura bitters
8 dashes orange citrate or bitters

Place all the ingredients in a vacuum bag and tightly seal the bag, squeezing out all the air (use a vacuum sealer if you have one). Place in a sous vide machine and hold in a 136°F/58°C bath for 4 hours. Remove from the machine, open the bag, decant the finished cocktail into 1 sealable bottle or a few smaller bottles, and chill until ready to serve. It will keep well for about 1 week. Pour the chilled cocktail over fresh ice.

NEGRONI

SIMPLE METHOD

INGREDIENTS

Serves 1

1½ ounces/40 ml gin
½ ounce/15 ml Martini Bitter vermouth
⅓ ounce/10 ml Martini Rosato
   vermouth

⅙ ounce/5 ml Cinzano Orancio
   vermouth
1 drop juniper extract
1 strip unwaxed orange peel

Pour all the ingredients except the orange peel into a mixing glass filled with ice cubes. Stir 25 times with a bar spoon, then strain and pour into a prechilled martini glass. Garnish with the orange peel.

PRO METHOD

INGREDIENTS

Serves 8

14 ounces/400 ml gin
5 ounces/150 ml Martini Bitter
   vermouth
3½ ounces/100 ml Martini Rosato
   vermouth

3½ ounces/100 ml still water
1¾ ounces/50 ml Cinzano Orancio
   vermouth

Place all the ingredients in a vacuum bag and tightly seal the bag, squeezing out all the air (use a vacuum sealer if you have one). Place in a sous vide machine and hold in a 136°F/58°C bath for 4 hours. Remove from the machine, open the bag, decant the finished cocktail into 1 sealable bottle or a few smaller bottles, and chill until ready to serve. It will keep well for about 1 week. Chill the martini glasses before serving.

VESPER

SIMPLE METHOD

INGREDIENTS

Serves 1

2 ounces/60 ml vodka
⅔ ounce/20 ml Lillet Blanc
3 drops juniper extract

1 drop lemon extract
1 drop Angostura bitters

Pour all the ingredients into a mixing glass filled with ice cubes. Stir 25 times with a bar spoon, then strain and pour over fresh ice in a rocks glass.

PRO METHOD

INGREDIENTS

Serves 8

20 ounces/600 ml vodka
7 ounces/200 ml Lillet Blanc
3½ ounces/100 ml still water

15 drops juniper extract
9 drops Angostura bitters
7 drops lemon extract

Place all the ingredients in a vacuum bag and tightly seal the bag, squeezing out all the air (use a vacuum sealer if you have one). Place in a sous vide machine and hold in a 136°F/58°C bath for 4 hours. Remove from the machine, open the bag, decant the finished cocktail into 1 sealable bottle or a few smaller bottles, and chill until ready to serve. It will keep well for about 1 week. If you want to serve your drink on the rocks, pour the chilled cocktail over fresh ice. Alternatively, chill the glasses before pouring.

MARTINEZ

SIMPLE METHOD

INGREDIENTS

Serves 1

1¾ ounces/50 ml gin
1 ounce/30 ml Carpano Antica
  Formula vermouth

3 dashes maraschino liqueur
1 strip unwaxed orange peel

Fill a mixing glass with ice cubes. Pour all the liquids into the glass and stir 25 times with a bar spoon. Strain into a prechilled martini glass and twist the orange peel above the glass until its oils have been released. Add the peel to the drink and serve.

PRO METHOD

INGREDIENTS

Serves 8

17 ounces/500 ml gin
10 ounces/300 ml Carpano Antica
  Formula vermouth
3½ ounces/100 ml maraschino liqueur
3½ ounces/100 ml still water

Peel of 2 unwaxed oranges
Peel of 2 unwaxed limes
Peel of 1 unwaxed lemon

Place all the ingredients in a vacuum bag and tightly seal the bag, squeezing out all the air (use a vacuum sealer if you have one). Place in a sous vide machine and hold in a 136°F/58°C bath for 4 hours. Remove from the machine, open the bag, decant the finished cocktail through a fine-mesh sieve into 1 sealable bottle or a few smaller bottles, and chill until ready to serve. It will keep well for about 1 week. Chill the martini glasses before serving.

MARTINI

Given the current fashion for almost eliminating vermouth from a martini, there is little point in recreating its flavor notes in a complex syrup. Rather, the art of the modern martini is to deliver the spirit alcohol (gin or vodka) at the perfect temperature, at a perfect dilution, and with a perfect viscosity. The key to all three is the ice. As a general rule, you want to add ½ to ⅔ ounce/15 to 20 ml of liquid (melted ice) to the cocktail through the process of stirring the drink. This brings the alcohol level down to a palatable level while chilling the drink. The second stirring also increases the density of the liquid, achieving the heaviness that we expect of a great martini. The skill is in knowing when to stop: continuing to stir past a certain point will result in overdilution.

INGREDIENTS

Serves 1

⅙ ounce/5 ml Noilly Prat vermouth
2 ounces/60 ml gin or vodka

1 strip unwaxed lemon peel,
  or 2 large green olives, pitted

Fill a mixing glass with ice cubes, then pour the vermouth over the ice. Stir 15 times with a bar spoon, then strain the ice, discarding the vermouth. Return the ice cubes to the glass. Pour the gin or vodka over the ice and stir a further 25 times. Strain into a prechilled martini glass and add the lemon peel to finish, allowing its oil to spread across the drink's surface. If you prefer olives, leave out the lemon and place the olives in the drink once poured.

DIRTY MARTINI

INGREDIENTS

Serves 1

4 large green olives, pitted
1/12 ounce/2.5 ml Noilly Prat vermouth
2 ounces/60 ml gin or vodka

Place 2 of the olives in a mixing glass and muddle until a paste forms. Fill the mixing glass with ice cubes, then dress the ice with the vermouth, followed by the gin or vodka. Stir 30 times with a bar spoon, then strain to remove the olive paste, pouring into a prechilled martini glass. Garnish with the remaining 2 olives.

OLD FASHIONED

SIMPLE METHOD

INGREDIENTS

Serves 1

1 sugar cube
2 dashes Angostura bitters

2 ounces/60 ml bourbon or whiskey
1 strip unwaxed orange peel

Place the sugar cube in a rocks glass and drip the bitters onto it, then crush the cube lightly with a bar spoon. Add 1 ounce/30 ml of the bourbon or whiskey and a handful of ice cubes and stir 20 times. Twist the orange peel over the glass until its oils are released, then add it to the glass. Add more ice and the remaining bourbon. Stir until the sugar has dissolved and serve.

PRO METHOD

INGREDIENTS

Serves 8

20 ounces/600 ml bourbon
7 ounces/200 ml still water

3½ ounces/100 ml Old Fashioned
  Sugar Syrup (below)
12 dashes Angostura bitters

Place all the ingredients in a vacuum bag and tightly seal the bag, squeezing out all the air (use a vacuum sealer if you have one). Place in a sous vide machine and hold in a 136°F/58°C bath for 4 hours. Remove from the machine, open the bag, decant the finished cocktail into 1 sealable bottle or a few smaller bottles, and chill until ready to serve. It will keep well for about 1 week. If you want to serve your drink on the rocks, pour the chilled cocktail over fresh ice. Alternatively, chill the glasses before pouring.

OLD FASHIONED SUGAR SYRUP

INGREDIENTS

Makes about 3½ cups/800 ml of syrup

2½ cups/500 g superfine sugar
¾ cup/250 g maple syrup
3 cups/750 ml still water
3 vanilla pods, split lengthwise

2 dried banana chips
4 star anise
6 cloves
1 cinnamon stick
Peel of 3 unwaxed oranges

Place all the ingredients in a wide saucepan and slowly bring to a boil. Simmer for 20 to 25 minutes without stirring. Remove from the heat and strain the syrup through cheesecloth into a clean sealable jar. Cool and chill. The syrup keeps well for 3 months.

SYRUPS & MACERATIONS

ONCE OR TWICE A WEEK at the Firehouse, a member of the bar team leads a "cooking day." The fragrances that emanate from the prep kitchen tell a story of seasonal fruits and Spice Route aromatics, and these become the syrups and macerations that underpin our cocktail menu.

Syrups and macerations also allow you to control the sugar content of your cocktails. Liqueurs, the old-fashioned method for delivering herb, nut, or spice notes to a cocktail, typically come with a penalty of overwhelming sweetness and of artificial flavors. Even fruit juices— the staple of 1980s cocktails—tend to add a lot of unwanted sugar for the amount of flavor they deliver. Simmering zest and peels in a sugar syrup, however, brings both more concentration of fruit flavor and a better balance of sugar.

Simmering zest and peels in a sugar syrup brings both more concentration of fruit flavor and a better balance of sugar.

An added bonus is that they freeze well and, as these recipes illustrate, create bases for a wide variety of cocktails. They elevate the art of cocktail making, capturing the flavors of a season's fruits. We suggest making several batches, in small quantities, when each fruit is at its in-season peak.

Think of it as jam-making with extra benefits.

STRAWBERRY-THYME SYRUP

This syrup, a vibrant blend of summer fruit and herbal aromatics, is best made with in-season strawberries and fresh thyme.

INGREDIENTS

Makes about 1 quart/1 liter syrup

5 cups/1 kg superfine sugar
1 quart/1 liter water

1 pound/500 g fresh strawberries
⅓ ounce/10 g fresh thyme

Put all the ingredients in a wide saucepan and place over medium heat. Bring to a boil, then reduce the heat and simmer for 10 to 15 minutes, uncovered, until the fruit is soft and falling apart. Do not stir. Remove from the heat and pass the mixture through a fine-mesh sieve into a clean heatproof container. Leave to cool, then chill or freeze. The syrup keeps well for 3 to 4 days in the fridge, or up to 6 months in the freezer.

STRAWBERRY SIGH

INGREDIENTS

Serves 1

½ ounce/15 ml vodka
½ ounce/15 ml Belsazar Rosé vermouth
⅔ ounce/20 ml Strawberry-Thyme
  Syrup (above)

2 drops grapefruit bitters
2⅓ ounces/70 ml champagne

Place all the ingredients except the champagne in a shaker. Fill the shaker with ice cubes, then cover and shake for 4 seconds. Strain through a cocktail strainer and pour into a prechilled flute. Finish with the champagne.

APPEARANCE OF VIRTUE

INGREDIENTS

Serves 1

FOR THE CHAMOMILE GIN:

⅓ ounce/10 g chamomile buds or
  good-quality chamomile tea leaves
A 750-ml bottle gin

FOR THE COCKTAIL:

1¾ ounces/50 ml chamomile gin
⅔ ounce/20 ml Lillet Rosé
½ ounce/15 ml Strawberry-Thyme Syrup
  (page 44)
1 strip unwaxed lemon peel
1 sprig thyme, to garnish

To make the chamomile gin, add the chamomile buds or tea leaves to the bottle of gin, seal, and leave to infuse at room temperature for 12 hours. Pass the gin through cheesecloth to remove the chamomile and transfer the infused gin back to the bottle. It will keep well for about 3 months at room temperature, or 6 months chilled.

Place all the ingredients for the cocktail, except the lemon peel and thyme, in a shaker. Fill the shaker with ice cubes, then cover and shake for 7 seconds. Strain through a cocktail strainer and pour into a prechilled martini glass. Twist the lemon peel over the drink to release its oils. Garnish with the lemon twist and thyme sprig.

COUNTRY MATTERS

INGREDIENTS

Serves 1

1½ ounces/45 ml gin
½ ounce/15 ml Strawberry-Thyme
  Syrup (page 44)
⅓ ounce/10 ml freshly squeezed
  lemon juice

3 drops mandarin bitters
2 drops vanilla bitters
⅔ ounce/20 ml soda water
1 sprig rosemary, to garnish

Place all the ingredients except the soda water and rosemary sprig in a shaker. Fill the shaker with ice cubes, then cover and shake for 3 seconds. Fill a highball glass with crushed ice and pour the liquid from the shaker over the ice. Gently top up the cocktail with soda. Using a cocktail spoon, carefully lift up the liquid from the bottom of the glass with a slow spiral movement to integrate the ingredients without damaging the soda bubbles. Garnish with the rosemary sprig.

BLUEBERRY-LAVENDER SYRUP

This wonderfully aromatic syrup is very delicate and versatile, with a bold floral top note, a fruity midpalate from the blueberries, and a lingering perfume from the elderflower. If fresh lavender is not available, dried lavender will work—just make sure that the lavender is labeled for culinary use.

INGREDIENTS

Makes about 3½ cups/800 ml syrup

5 cups/1 kg superfine sugar
1 quart/1 liter water
25 fresh sprigs lavender,
  or ½ ounce/15 g dried lavender

Peel from 1 unwaxed lemon
14 ounces/400 g fresh blueberries
⅔ ounce/20 ml elderflower cordial

Add the sugar, water, lavender, and lemon peel to a wide saucepan and place over medium heat. Bring to a boil, then reduce the heat. Add the blueberries and elderflower cordial and bring back to a boil. Reduce the heat and simmer for 10 to 15 minutes, uncovered, until the fruit is soft and falling apart. Do not stir. Remove from the heat and pass the mixture through cheesecloth into a clean heatproof container. Leave to cool, then chill or freeze. The syrup keeps well for 3 to 4 days in the fridge, or up to 6 months in the freezer.

CHILTERN AVIATION

INGREDIENTS

Serves 1

1½ ounces/45 ml gin (an aromatic gin
  with forward juniper notes—ideally a
  London Dry—works best)
½ ounce/15 ml Luxardo maraschino
  liqueur

⅓ ounce/10 ml Blueberry-Lavender
  Syrup (above)
⅔ ounce/20 ml freshly squeezed
  lemon juice
1 strip unwaxed lemon peel

Place all the ingredients except the lemon peel in a shaker. Fill the shaker with ice cubes, then cover and shake for 7 seconds. Strain through a cocktail strainer and pour into a prechilled martini glass. Twist the lemon peel over the drink to release its oils, then discard.

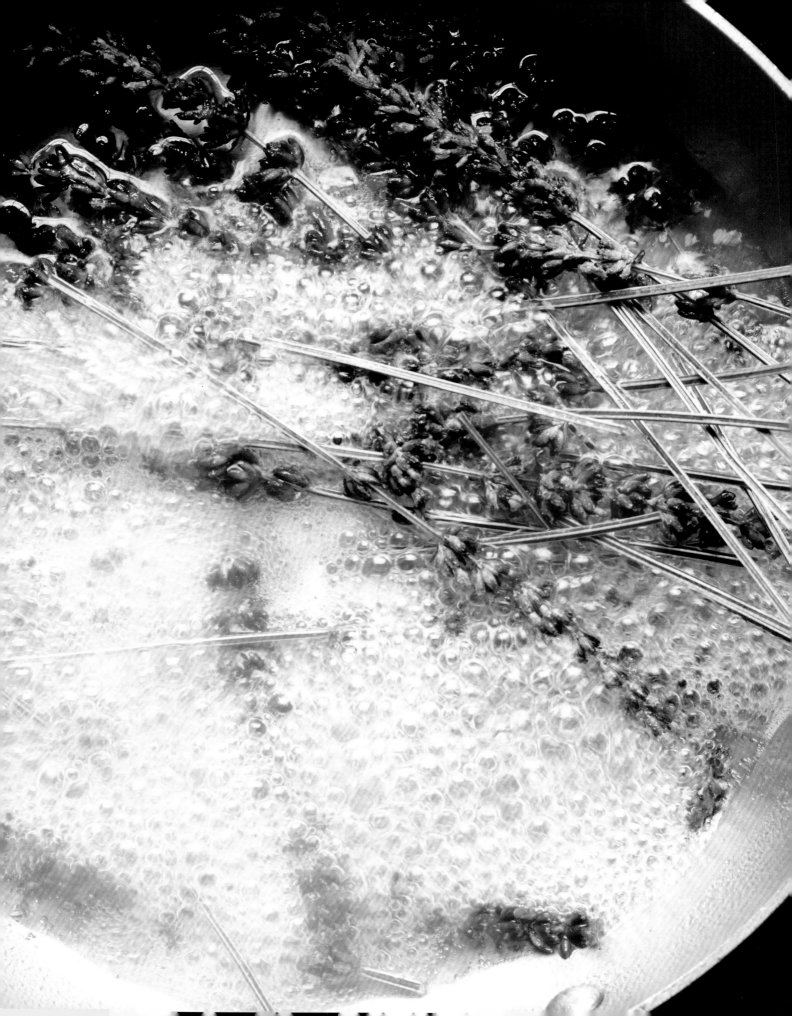

SEX AND VIOLETS

INGREDIENTS

Serves 1

⅓ ounce/10 ml Blueberry-Lavender
  Syrup (page 50)
⅙ ounce/5 ml elderflower cordial

2¾ ounces/80 ml champagne

Place the syrup and cordial in a shaker. Fill the shaker with ice cubes, then cover and shake for 4 seconds. Strain through a cocktail strainer and pour into a prechilled flute. Finish with the champagne.

PROMENADE DES ANGLAIS

INGREDIENTS

Serves 1

FOR THE HERB-INFUSED GIN:

5 teaspoons dried herbes de Provence
A 1-liter bottle gin

FOR THE COCKTAIL:

1⅓ ounces/40 ml herb-infused gin
½ ounce/15 ml Dolin de Chambery
  Blanc vermouth
½ ounce/15 ml Blueberry-Lavender
  Syrup (page 50)
¼ ounce/7.5 ml freshly squeezed
  lemon juice
1 strip unwaxed lemon peel

To make the herb-infused gin, add the dried herbes de Provence to the bottle of gin, seal, and leave to infuse at room temperature for 3 hours. Pass the gin through cheesecloth to remove the herbs and transfer the infused gin back to the bottle. It will keep well for about 3 months at room temperature, or 6 months chilled.

Place all the ingredients for the cocktail, except the lemon peel, in a shaker. Fill the shaker with ice cubes, then cover and shake for 7 seconds. Strain through a cocktail strainer and pour into a prechilled martini glass. Finish by rubbing the lemon peel on the rim of the glass and adding the peel to the cocktail.

CLOCKWISE FROM TOP LEFT:
SEX AND VIOLETS,
CHILTERN AVIATION (PAGE 50),
PROMENADE DES ANGLAIS

NUT SYRUP

This luscious syrup has a buttery, almost caramel undertone and a burst of spices and nut flavors on the finish. The maple syrup adds smokiness and the chocolate a lasting note of bittersweet richness. Make sure to use fresh nuts—the nuts in a package that has been open for more than 1 month will have started to lose their freshness.

INGREDIENTS

Makes about 2 cups/500 ml syrup

2¼ cups/700 g maple syrup
¾ cup/200 ml water
1¾ ounces/50 g almonds
1¾ ounces/50 g hazelnuts

1¾ ounces/50 g walnuts
1 teaspoon freshly grated nutmeg
2 vanilla pods
4 to 5 drops chocolate extract

Put all the ingredients in a wide saucepan and place over medium heat. Bring to a boil, then reduce the heat and simmer, uncovered, for 10 to 15 minutes. Do not stir. Remove from the heat and pass the mixture through a fine-mesh sieve into a clean heatproof container. Leave to cool, then chill or freeze. The syrup keeps well for 3 to 4 days in the fridge, or up to 6 months in the freezer.

FIREHOUSE SAZERAC

INGREDIENTS

Serves 1

⅙ ounce/5 ml absinthe
1¼ ounces/35 ml Cognac
1¼ ounces/35 ml rye whiskey
½ ounce/15 ml Nut Syrup (above)

2 dashes Angostura bitters
2 dashes Creole bitters
1 strip unwaxed lemon peel

Fill a brandy glass with ice cubes and add the absinthe. Stir until the glass is well frosted, then set aside. Place the remaining ingredients, except the lemon peel, into a mixing glass and fill with ice cubes. Stir 25 times. Discard the absinthe-coated ice from the brandy glass and add an ice block or ice ball. Strain the drink over the ice. Twist the lemon peel over the glass to release its oils then add it to the cocktail.

CHARMED AND DANGEROUS

INGREDIENTS

Serves 1

1½ ounces/45 ml single-malt whiskey
½ ounce/15 ml Maury sweet wine
⅓ ounce/10 ml Nut Syrup (page 54)

2 dashes Spanish bitters
1 strip unwaxed orange peel
1 strip unwaxed lime peel (optional)

Place all the ingredients except the lime peel in a mixing glass. Fill the glass with ice cubes and stir 25 times. Strain through a cocktail strainer and pour into a prechilled rocks glass half-filled with fresh ice cubes. Rub the rim of the glass with the lime peel and discard.

LOVER'S SPLIFF

INGREDIENTS

Serves 1

½ ounce/15 ml amber rum
⅓ ounce/10 ml Nut Syrup (page 54)
1 thin slice fresh ginger
2 thin slices fresh pear

3 drops chocolate bitters
2¾ ounces/80 ml champagne
1 sprig lavender (optional)

Place all the ingredients except the champagne and lavender in a shaker. Fill the shaker with ice cubes then cover and shake for 4 seconds. Strain through a cocktail strainer and pour into a prechilled flute. Finish with champagne and garnish with the sprig of lavender.

STORY OF O

INGREDIENTS

Serves 1

1¼ ounces/35 ml gin
½ ounce/15 ml apricot brandy
½ ounce/15 ml Nut Syrup (page 54)
⅔ ounce/20 ml fresh lime juice

2 dashes Angostura bitters
1 strip unwaxed lime peel
1 sprig lemon thyme (optional)

Place all the ingredients except the lime peel and lemon thyme in a shaker. Fill the shaker with ice cubes then cover and shake for 10 seconds. Strain through a cocktail strainer and pour into a rocks glass half-filled with fresh ice (ideally a single, large ice ball). Twist the lime peel over the drink to release its oils and add it to the drink. Garnish with the sprig of lemon thyme.

LEFT: LOVER'S SPLIFF
RIGHT: STORY OF O

APPLE, VANILLA, AND BAY SYRUP

This is our most complex syrup. Gently caramelizing the apples in the sugar is the key, yielding a honeyed, treacly flavor, balanced by notes of vanilla, pepper, and bay. For a more Christmas-y note, add half a stick of cinnamon.

INGREDIENTS

Makes about 1 quart/1 liter syrup

5 cups/1 kg superfine sugar
2 green apples, coarsely chopped
  (peel and core intact)
1 quart/1 liter water

10 fresh or 5 dried bay leaves
¼ vanilla pod, split lengthwise
2 tablespoons crushed black
  peppercorns
1 cinnamon stick (optional)
Pinch Maldon sea salt

Place the sugar and apples in a wide saucepan over low heat and cook gently, stirring occasionally with a wooden spoon, until the sugar dissolves and the apples start to caramelize. Add all the remaining ingredients, increase the heat, and simmer for 10 to 15 minutes. Do not stir. Remove from the heat and pass the mixture through a fine-mesh sieve into a heatproof container. Leave to cool, then chill or freeze. The syrup keeps well for 3 to 4 days in the fridge, or up to 6 months in the freezer.

EDEN'S APPLE

INGREDIENTS

Serves 1

1⅓ ounces/40 ml vodka
⅓ ounce/10 ml calvados
⅓ ounce/10 ml Cocchi Americano
  vermouth

⅓ ounce/10 ml Apple, Vanilla,
  and Bay Syrup (above)
2 drops Burlesque bitters
1 bay leaf

Place all the ingredients except the bay leaf in a mixing glass. Fill the mixing glass with equal parts ice cubes and crushed ice. Stir 25 times. Strain through a cocktail strainer and pour into a prechilled coupe glass. Garnish with the bay leaf.

DASHAMOUR

INGREDIENTS

Serves 1

4 thin slices jalapeño pepper
2 strips lime peel
1¾ ounces/50 ml tequila reposado
⅔ ounce/20 ml Martini Rosato
  vermouth

⅓ ounce/10 ml Domaine Canton
  ginger liqueur
¼ ounce/7.5 ml Apple, Vanilla,
  and Bay Syrup (page 59)
6 dashes Hellfire bitters

Place 2 of the jalapeño slices in a mixing glass and muddle with a bar spoon or muddler. Fill the mixing glass with ice cubes and twist one of the strips of lime peel over the glass to release its oils before adding to the glass.

Add all ingredients except the second strip of lime peel and remaining 2 jalapeño slices to the glass and stir 25 times. Strain into a rocks glass filled with fresh ice (ideally, one large cube). To finish, twist the second strip of lime peel over the drink to release its oils, and then use as a garnish together with the remaining 2 jalapeño slices.

Note: The 6 dashes of Hellfire bitters will yield a drink with considerable heat. Adjust the number of dashes according to individual preference. The Apple, Vanilla, and Bay syrup nicely mellows out the drink, but unless you have a batch made, it is not a vital ingredient, as the jalapeño, ginger liqueur, and lime all contribute strong flavors.

LIVING IN SIN

INGREDIENTS

Serves 1

1¾ ounces/50 ml Japanese
  blended whiskey
⅔ ounce/20 ml Tintilla de Rota*
⅓ ounce/10 ml Apple, Vanilla,
  and Bay Syrup (page 59)

½ teaspoon honey, ideally truffle honey
4 drops chocolate bitters
1 strip unwaxed lemon peel

Place all the ingredients except the lemon peel in a mixing glass. Fill the mixing glass with ice cubes and stir 25 times. Strain through a cocktail strainer and pour into a prechilled rocks glass half-filled with fresh ice cubes. Twist the lemon peel over the glass to release its oils and add it to the cocktail.

Tintilla de Rota is a fortified red wine from the sherry region of Spain. A Banyuls from southern France would work equally well. Both wines pair beautifully with rich cheeses and chocolate, should you have some left over.

CHERRY MACERATION

Macerations are not cooked, but left to steep and develop flavors over a long period of time. The principal requirement here is patience: you really do need to leave it for at least a month, in a cool, dry place—it will taste even better after 2 or 3 months, and will keep well for up to 6 months. Sterilizing the jar just before adding the ingredients is essential.

INGREDIENTS

Makes about 3½ cups/800 ml

20 ounces/600 ml bourbon
5 ounces/150 ml orange Curaçao
5 ounces/150 ml Luxardo
  maraschino liqueur
4⅓ pounds/2 kg whole fresh cherries

3½ ounces/100 ml still water
3 vanilla pods, split lengthwise
2 cinnamon sticks
Peel of 5 unwaxed oranges

Sterilize a 3-quart/3-liter mason jar, or several smaller jars, by placing the jar (or jars) in a sink and filling them with boiling water, also pouring some of the boiling water over the inside of the lids. Let them sit for 5 minutes, then drain.

Place all the ingredients in the jar or jars (dividing the ingredients equally between the jars), stir several times with a sterilized long spoon, and seal. When using the maceration, just pour the required amount through a sieve, then reseal the jar.

CHERRY BABY

INGREDIENTS

Serves 1

1 strawberry, hulled
1⅓ ounces/40 ml tequila
⅓ ounce/10 ml Martini Fiero vermouth

⅔ ounce/20 ml Cherry Maceration
  (above)
½ teaspoon balsamic vinegar
½ teaspoon fennel seeds

Place the strawberry in a mixing glass, muddle with a bar spoon or muddler, then fill the glass with ice cubes and add the remaining ingredients. Stir 25 times. Strain through a cocktail strainer into a prechilled rocks glass half-filled with fresh ice cubes.

BAISE-EN-VILLE

INGREDIENTS

Serves 1

1 Luxardo maraschino cherry
1 strip unwaxed orange peel
1¼ ounces/35 ml bourbon
½ ounce/15 ml Martini Rosso vermouth

⅔ ounce/20 ml Cherry Maceration
 (page 62)
1 dash orange bitters
1 strip unwaxed lemon peel

Place the Luxardo cherry in a mixing glass and muddle with a bar spoon or muddler. Fill the mixing glass with ice cubes and twist the orange peel over the glass to release its oils, then place the twist in the glass. Add all the ingredients, except the lemon peel, to the glass with the muddled cherry and stir 25 times. Strain into a prechilled martini glass. To finish, twist the lemon peel over the drink to release its oils, then discard.

BLACK CHERRY MANHATTAN

INGREDIENTS

Serves 1

1½ ounces/45 ml bourbon
1¼ ounces/35 ml Noilly Rouge vermouth
⅔ ounce/20 ml Cherry Maceration
 (page 62)

2 drops Angostura bitters
1 drop orange citrate or bitters
1 strip unwaxed orange peel
1 Luxardo maraschino cherry

Place all the ingredients except the orange peel in a mixing glass. Fill the mixing glass with ice cubes and stir 25 times. Strain through a cocktail strainer, pour into a prechilled martini glass, and garnish with the orange peel and cherry.

CHERRY DROP

INGREDIENTS

Serves 1

⅔ ounce/20 ml gin
⅓ ounce/10 ml Vergano Luli Chinato
 vermouth
1⅓ ounces/40 ml Cherry Maceration
 (page 62)

1 teaspoon maple syrup
1 strip unwaxed orange peel
Splash of ginger beer

Place all the ingredients except the orange peel and ginger beer in a mixing glass. Fill the mixing glass with ice cubes and stir 25 times. Strain through a cocktail strainer into a prechilled rocks glass half-filled with fresh ice cubes. Rub the rim of the glass with the orange peel then add to the drink. Finish with a splash of ginger beer.

BLACK CHERRY
MANHATTAN

APERITIVI

VERMOUTHS ARE THE AROMATIC HEART of modern mixology. With their constellation of flavor notes— fruits, bark, herbs, roots, and botanicals, in multiple (and always secret) combinations, running the spectrum from dry to sweet—they bring depth and harmony to almost any drink. We carry more than fifty different vermouths at the Firehouse, from producers large and small, a selection that grew from a desire to share our passion with our guests, and to push beyond the traditional vermouth on rocks.

Our bar menu describes them as "lightly enhanced vermouths," though they could also be called hybrid cocktails; as in creating a cocktail, the method was to enhance primary flavors in the alcohol and to add a complementary counterpoint—a sprig of lavender, a light dusting of black pepper.

With their constellation of flavor notes, they bring depth and harmony to almost any drink.

These are essentially summer drinks, to be enjoyed at lunch or before dinner. Their low alcohol content makes them an ideal precursor to drinking wine, and their simple, refreshing flavors prepare the palate for a meal.

MELA

LAVANDA

INGREDIENTS

Serves 1

1¾ ounces/50 ml Belsazar dry
  vermouth
1 sprig lemon thyme
1 strip unwaxed lemon peel
1 sprig fresh lavender

Add the vermouth and lemon thyme sprig to a mixing glass and lightly macerate
with a muddler. Fill the glass with ice cubes and stir 20 times. Strain through a cocktail
strainer and pour into a rocks glass half-filled with fresh ice cubes. Garnish with the
lemon peel and lavender sprig.

MELA

INGREDIENTS

Serves 1

8 thin slices green apple
3 basil leaves
1¾ ounces/50 ml Lillet Blanc vermouth

Muddle 4 slices of the apple in a mixing glass until lightly crushed. Fill with ice cubes.
Add 1 basil leaf and the vermouth. Stir 20 times. Strain through a cocktail strainer and
pour into a rocks glass half-filled with fresh ice cubes. Rub the used basil leaf around
the rim of the glass and discard. Garnish with the remaining apple slices and fresh
basil leaves.

FRESA

INGREDIENTS

Serves 1

2 strawberries, hulled
  and cut into quarters

1¾ ounces/50 ml Martini D'Oro
  vermouth
2 sprigs lemon balm

Add the strawberries, vermouth, and 1 lemon balm sprig to a mixing glass and lightly
macerate with a muddler. Fill the glass with ice cubes and stir 20 times. Strain and pour
into a rocks glass half-filled with fresh ice cubes. Garnish with the remaining lemon
balm sprig.

ROSA

INGREDIENTS

Serves 1

1 thin slice fresh ginger
1 raspberry
7 rose petals

1¾ ounces/50 ml Cocchi Americano
  Rosa vermouth
1 drop Hellfire bitters
Freshly ground black pepper

Muddle the ginger and raspberry in a mixing glass until lightly crushed. Fill with ice cubes. Add 2 rose petals, the vermouth, and bitters. Stir 20 times. Strain through a cocktail strainer into a rocks glass half-filled with fresh ice. Finish with a light dusting of freshly ground black pepper and the remaining rose petals.

ARANCIONE

INGREDIENTS

Serves 1

1¾ ounces/50 ml Martini Bitter vermouth
1 drop vanilla bitters
1 strip unwaxed orange peel

Fill a mixing glass with ice cubes. Add the vermouth and vanilla bitters. Stir 20 times. Strain through a cocktail strainer and pour into a rocks glass half-filled with fresh ice. Twist the orange peel over the glass to release its oils, and add it to drink.

LIMONE

INGREDIENTS

Serves 1

1 cherry, pitted
1¾ ounces/50 ml Dolin Rouge
  vermouth
½ ounce/15 ml Cocchi Americano
  vermouth

½ ounce/15 ml Acqua di Cedro
  lemon liqueur
2 drops orange bitters
1 strip unwaxed Amalfi lemon peel

Add the pitted cherry to a mixing glass and lightly muddle. Fill the glass with ice cubes. Add the vermouths, lemon liqueur, and orange bitters and stir 20 times. Strain through a cocktail strainer and pour into a rocks glass half-filled with fresh ice. Twist the lemon peel over the glass to release its oils, and add it to the drink.

ROSA

SNACKS

CRAB DOUGHNUTS

These lovely morsels came about when a friend came to visit and I wanted to serve a nice snack with his drinks one night. In my restaurant at the time, we were serving brown crab doughnuts dusted with crab coral and a spiced mix of sugar and salt. But this time, we fried a couple of pieces of doughnut and stuffed them with a creamy, spiced fresh crabmeat mix. He liked them very much, and although we didn't make them together again, the idea stuck with me and they became a signature dish at the Firehouse. To this day my friend probably still doesn't know that he was the first person to try them!

During my time in North America I fell in love with many street food dishes that combined ethnic cuisines with American staples. The style of doughnut we use here is inspired by a Chinese fried bread recipe using an American-style creamy crabmeat mix as a stuffing. At the Firehouse we merge the sweet, savory, and spicy flavors together by dusting the doughnuts with a mixture of confectioner's sugar with crab coral and dehydrated tomato oil.

Make plenty because they disappear fast!

NUNO'S TIP

The quantity of doughnut dough will give you more doughnuts than you need. The leftover dough can be cut into 2-inch/ 5-cm circles and deep-fried until golden brown, then coated in sugar for a quick treat. The doughnut is a perfect vehicle for any type of filling or dip:

Roll them in vanilla-cinnamon sugar as soon as they come out of the deep-fat fryer. Serve them with a vanilla pastry cream custard flavored with the grated zest of an orange and a lemon and spiked with aged rum.

A savory alternative is to cook a mix of Japanese mushrooms with rosemary, butter, mirin, and soy sauce, chop them into a coarse paste, stuff the doughnuts with the mix, and dust them with dehydrated ground black trumpet mushroom mixed together with confectioner's sugar, salt, and five-spice powder (3 parts confectioner's sugar to 1 part salt and 1 part five-spice).

INGREDIENTS

Makes 8 doughnuts

FOR THE DOUGHNUTS:

3¾ cups/540 g white bread flour, plus extra to dust
6 tablespoons/70 g superfine sugar
2 teaspoons Maldon sea salt, plus 1 tablespoon to dust
1 teaspoon instant yeast
½ cup plus 2 tablespoons/140 ml water, at room temperature
4 large free-range eggs
Grated zest of 3 unwaxed lemons
9 tablespoons/130 g unsalted butter, thinly sliced and chilled
2 cups/500 ml sunflower oil, for deep frying, plus extra for greasing

3 tablespoons confectioner's sugar, to dust
1 tablespoon ground cinnamon, to dust

FOR THE TOMATO JUICE:

5 beefsteak tomatoes, or the largest variety you can find
1 clove garlic, chopped
½ shallot, chopped
⅛ red chile, seeded and chopped
1½ teaspoons sherry vinegar
1½ teaspoons fish sauce
Maldon sea salt, to taste

CONTINUED

FOR THE CRAB DOUGHNUT
FILLING:

7 ounces/200 g picked white crab meat
  (from the claws)
2 tablespoons tomato juice
  (previous page)

2 tablespoons crème fraîche
1 tablespoon thinly sliced basil leaves
2½ teaspoons freshly squeezed
  lemon juice
Maldon sea salt to taste

MAKE THE DOUGHNUTS

Place the flour, sugar, salt and yeast in the bowl of a stand mixer fitted with the dough hook attachment and mix at low speed. In a separate bowl, combine the water, eggs, and lemon zest.

Slowly add the liquid mixture to the flour mixture with the mixer at low speed until it forms a dough. Increase the speed and knead for 10 to 12 minutes, until the dough comes away from the sides of the bowl and is smooth and elastic.

Reduce the speed to low and add the butter a slice at a time. Once all the butter has been incorporated, increase the speed, and knead for a further 5 to 6 minutes, until you have a smooth dough. You can make the dough by hand, but you need to work quickly to make sure the dough doesn't get too warm.

Cover the bowl with plastic wrap and place in the fridge for at least 6 hours or overnight, to allow the dough to rest and rise slowly. The next day, oil a baking sheet. Roll the dough to a ¾ inch/2 cm thickness on a lightly floured work surface and cut out eight 1¼-inch/3-cm circles. Roll each circle into a ball and place them on the oiled baking sheet. Cover and leave to rise for 2 to 3 hours.

Pour the sunflower oil into a deep saucepan or deep-fat fryer with (so it's roughly half-filled with oil), and place over medium heat until it reaches 350°F/175°C. Deep-fry the doughnuts, four at a time, for 2 to 3 minutes, basting them constantly with the oil until they are golden brown. Transfer to a plate lined with paper towels to drain.

MAKE THE TOMATO JUICE

Cut the tomatoes in half and squeeze out the seeds. Grate the flesh of the tomatoes on the side of a box grater over a bowl. Place the grated tomato flesh in the bowl of a food processor with the remaining ingredients and blend until smooth, or use a stick blender. Transfer the mixture to a muslin cloth and hang the cloth over a bowl for 2 hours.

**MAKE THE CRAB
DOUGHNUT FILLING**

Combine all the ingredients in a bowl and mix well. Cover and chill until ready to assemble.

ASSEMBLE & SERVE

Cut each doughnut in half and fill it with the chilled crab mixture. Mix the confectioner's sugar in a bowl with the cinnamon and salt and dust the doughnuts with the mix. Serve immediately (the doughnuts won't keep for long once filled).

CAULIFLOWER FLORETS WITH TRUFFLE PURÉE

This snack is based around the concept of crudités. I have always enjoyed a raw, crunchy vegetable served with a dip at the start of a meal. It is a healthy and fun way to fire up your taste buds. We've played with the classic combination of cauliflower and truffle and created this dish, where the flavor and texture of the cauliflower and the earthy, rich truffle stand side by side in perfect harmony.

For a quick upgrade, enhance the dish with gratings of fresh truffle.

In the restaurant we serve it as a starter with 5 to 6 florets per person, but the recipe also makes an ideal party canapé. Leftovers make a perfect garnish for a piece of sea bass or salmon.

INGREDIENTS

Serves 4 as a snack or starter,
or 10 as a canapé

1 tablespoon salt
Vegetable oil, for deep-frying
1 whole cauliflower, cut into
 small bite-sized florets, leaves
 and trimmings retained

FOR THE BROWN BUTTER
CRUMBS:

⅞ cup/200 g unsalted butter
⅓ cup/50 g dry milk

FOR THE CAULIFLOWER &
TRUFFLE PURÉE:

2 tablespoons melted butter (from
 making the brown butter crumbs)
4 ounces/125 g cauliflower trimmings
 (left from your whole cauliflower—
 the stem, core, and floret trimmings)
2½ tablespoons whole milk,
 plus extra if necessary
1⅓ ounces/40 g truffle paste
1½ teaspoons cider vinegar

CONTINUED

BRINE THE CAULIFLOWER & FRY THE CAULIFLOWER LEAVES

Dissolve the salt in a saucepan with 1 quart/1 liter of warm water and leave to cool to room temperature.

While the brine is cooling, fill a deep saucepan two-thirds full with vegetable oil and heat to 300°F/150°C. Fry the cauliflower leaves for 2 minutes, until crispy, then remove from the oil and transfer to paper towels to drain. Tidy the edges of the leaves to make them presentable and easy to pick up.

Drop the cauliflower florets into the brine and leave them at room temperature for 2 hours (in the restaurant we use a vacuum sealer to force the brine inside the cauliflower and season the pieces all the way through), then drain.

MAKE THE BROWN BUTTER CRUMBS

Have a sieve on hand, and a pan and paper towels ready on the work surface. Melt the butter in a saucepan over medium heat. Whisk in the dry milk and continue to cook for about 4 minutes, until the mixture turns nut brown. As soon as the mixture is ready (be careful not to let it burn) strain it through a fine-mesh sieve into the pan. Transfer the milk crumbs in the sieve to paper towels, changing the paper towels a few times until the crumbs are dry and crisp. Divide between two airtight containers once cool, and set to one side until ready to use.

MAKE THE CAULIFLOWER & TRUFFLE PURÉE

Place the melted butter, cauliflower trimmings, and milk in a small saucepan, cover, and cook over low heat for 10 to 15 minutes, until the cauliflower is completely softened. Transfer the mixture to the bowl of a food processor or blender and process until you have a smooth purée, adding a little more milk if necessary. Mix in the truffle paste, vinegar, and ½ ounce/15 g of the brown butter crumbs.

SERVE

Pipe or spoon some of the truffle purée into a serving bowl, place the drained florets in the bowl, with the stems pointing up to make them easier to pick up, then scatter with the remaining brown butter crumbs. Add the fried cauliflower leaves to the bowl, slotted between the florets. Repeat with the remaining servings.

SPICED VENISON PUFFS

We once made spiced venison puffs for our neighbors at the Chiltern Street Christmas Party and they were so tasty that we decided to keep them on the menu as a snack from Thanksgiving until Christmas.

This recipe is a merging of two bite-sized treats: sausage rolls, a traditional British snack, and one of my favorite baked dim sum—*char siu so* (sweet pork). They are fun to make and great to nibble on during the festive season.

This recipe also works well with a spiced prawn béchamel stuffing. Roast prawn heads and shells, then add to milk with lots of fried garlic and cilantro and leave to infuse for 2 hours. Make a classic béchamel with flour and butter, gradually stirring in the infused milk. Finish the béchamel with chopped cooked prawns, chopped cilantro, and a splash of cognac. Make the mix quite thick and chunky. Allow it to cool down before folding it in pastry like a sealed dumpling and baking as directed.

INGREDIENTS

Serves 6 to 8

FOR THE PUFF PASTRY:

4¼ cups/600 g very strong white high-protein flour, preferably 00, plus extra to dust
1¾ ounces/50 g unsmoked pork fat or lard
Pinch salt
Pinch five-spice powder, briefly toasted in a dry frying pan
Pinch ground white pepper
2 tablespoons red wine vinegar
A scant cup/230 ml ice-cold water
1¾ cups/400 g cold unsalted butter

FOR THE VENISON FILLING:

2 tablespoons grapeseed oil
2 shallots, thinly diced
10 fresh shiitake mushrooms, stems removed and caps thinly diced
2 teaspoons ground white pepper

2 teaspoons five-spice powder, briefly toasted in a dry frying pan
5 green onions, thinly sliced
5 water chestnuts, thinly chopped
Bunch of chives, thinly snipped
17 ounces/500 g minced venison (preferably shoulder)
3½ ounces/100 g smoked pork fat (Lardo di Colonnata), grated
4 tablespoons low-salt soy sauce
2 tablespoons honey
2 tablespoons sriracha
2 tablespoons hoisin sauce
2 pinches Maldon sea salt

TO FINISH:

2 large free-range eggs, beaten, for egg wash
Toasted white sesame seeds, for sprinkling
Smoked ketchup, to serve (optional)

MAKE THE PUFF PASTRY (IDEALLY THE DAY BEFORE COOKING)

This is a classic puff pastry technique that you can use for many other recipes at home (minus the spices and vinegar, and replacing the pork fat with unsalted butter).

Sift the flour into a large bowl. Melt the pork fat or lard in a saucepan, then add the salt, spices, vinegar, and ice-cold water and combine. Add the mixture to the flour and stir to form a smooth dough. Wrap in plastic wrap and chill for 1 hour.

Slice the butter lengthwise into ½-inch/1-cm-thick pieces and lay them evenly over a small sheet of greaseproof paper. Cover with a second sheet of greaseproof paper and roll out gently to an even ¼ inch/5 mm thickness. Remove the pastry from the fridge and roll it out on a lightly floured surface to a rectangle just over twice the size of the butter. Remove the butter from the greaseproof paper and place it in the middle of the pastry. Make an envelope around the butter with the pastry, totally encasing it. Roll out the pastry again to a rectangle the same size as it was before the butter was added, then fold it 3 times, like a letter. Roll it out once more, turning it 90 degrees and folding it 3 times again. Wrap in plastic wrap and chill for 1 hour. Repeat the rolling and folding 4 more times, adding a light dusting of flour to the work surface each time, and chilling in the fridge after each repetition. During this process, it is important to make sure that the butter never melts. As friction from the rolling pin heats up the butter you need to cool it often or the layers of puff pastry will not puff up well. Be careful not to break the layers if they get too thin. Repeat this process 5 or 6 times (a minimum of 10 rolling, folding and chilling sequences). The more times you roll it and fold it, the more flaky layers you will have once it's baked. Wrap the pastry in plastic wrap and leave it to rest in the fridge overnight.

MAKE THE VENISON FILLING

Heat the grapeseed oil in a saucepan over medium heat, add the shallots and shiitake mushrooms, and sauté for 2 minutes, then add the ground white pepper and five-spice powder and sauté for a further 2 minutes, until the spices are fragrant and the shallots softened. Remove from the heat, add the green onions, water chestnuts, and chives and mix well.

In a large bowl, thoroughly combine the minced venison, grated pork fat, soy sauce, honey, sriracha, and hoisin along with the vegetable mixture (use your hands if you wish). Season with the salt. To check the seasoning, fry a small spoonful of the mixture in a frying pan on both sides and taste. Adjust seasoning accordingly, if you prefer more spice or salt. Cover the bowl with plastic wrap and chill until required.

ASSEMBLE & COOK THE PUFFS

Preheat the oven to 350°F/180°C. Roll out the pastry on a lightly floured surface to form a ¼-inch/5-mm-thick rectangle, and spoon on the mix, placing it in a line along the length of the pastry. Enclose to make a classic sausage roll shape and seal the edges to contain the filling. Brush the top liberally with egg wash, cut into 1¼-inch/3-cm lengths, and sprinkle generously with the toasted sesame seeds.

Transfer to a lined baking sheet and bake for 20 to 25 minutes, until puffed and golden brown. Remove from the oven and serve immediately, while still warm, with smoked ketchup if you like.

If you have leftover filling, freeze it to use at a later date, or roll it into sausages, dip in flour, then egg wash, then bread crumbs and fry to make venison croquettes.

BACON CORNBREAD FINGERS WITH CHIPOTLE MAPLE BUTTER

Wow, these guys are very special! Inspired by my time in New Mexico, these are baked in a madeleine pan, to bear a passing resemblance to cornbreads I baked in corn-shaped cast-iron molds with my chef and friend Mark Miller, in whose restaurant—Coyote Café in Santa Fe—I worked in 2002. Cooking with him was one of the most inspiring times in my career; I truly learned a new language of cooking and ingredients when I set foot in his kitchen, and I fell in love with Latin American cuisines. His knowledge of Latin American flavors, ingredients, and techniques is almost unrivaled, and his influence is still present in my cooking. Our Firehouse recipe is very different but I preserved the similar shape as a tribute to Mark and his passion.

The cornbreads must always be baked just before serving. They taste wonderful right out of the oven. Even if you choose not to make the chipotle butter and serve them with plain butter or seasoned sour cream they are still special. If you make a large batch of batter, chill it and use the rest the next day.

If you want go super decadent, serve the warm cornbread with thick-cut slices of smoked salmon, seasoned crème fraîche, thinly snipped chives, and an iced jar of caviar. Make sure you also bring a bottle of vintage Champagne to the party!

INGREDIENTS

Makes 24 madeleine-sized cornbreads,
or 6 portions (4 per person)

FOR THE CORNBREAD:

⅔ cup/150 g unsalted butter,
  plus extra for greasing
1¾ ounces/50 g bacon fat or lard
1⅜ cups/200 g all-purpose flour
1 cup/200 g superfine sugar
1½ teaspoons salt
Pinch cayenne pepper
1½ teaspoons baking powder
3 large free-range eggs
4 teaspoons maple syrup
2 teaspoons truffle paste
¾ cup/120 g frozen corn
5 chives, snipped
3 sprigs tarragon, leaves picked
  and chopped

FOR THE CHIPOTLE
MAPLE BUTTER:

2 cups/480 g unsalted butter,
  softened a little
5 tablespoons/100 g maple syrup
1 tablespoon chipotle paste
1 teaspoon Maldon sea salt
Pinch freshly ground black pepper

2 ounces/60 g tortilla chips, crumbled,
  to serve

CONTINUED

MAKE THE CORNBREAD

Place the butter and bacon fat in a pan and let it melt gently over low heat. Remove from the heat and set aside. Mix the flour, sugar, salt, cayenne, and baking powder together in a bowl.

In a separate bowl, whisk the eggs, maple syrup, and truffle paste until combined. Mix the egg mixture into the flour mixture. Blend the frozen corn in a blender or the bowl of a food processor to form medium-fine crumbs, then stir it into the egg and flour mixture. Fold the melted butter and fat into the mixture, a little at a time, so that the mixture doesn't split and curdle. Fold in the herbs, cover, and leave to rest in the fridge for at least 4 hours (but no longer than 12 hours).

Brush two 12-hole madeleine molds with melted butter and preheat the oven to 350°F/180°C. Pipe or spoon the batter into the madeleine molds, until each hole is three-quarters full. Bake for 12 to 14 minutes, turning the pans midway through baking to ensure they're evenly baked, until cooked through, with a golden-brown crust. A toothpick inserted into one of the madeleines should come out clean.

MAKE THE CHIPOTLE MAPLE BUTTER

Place the butter in a bowl and add the remaining ingredients. Beat the mixture, either in a stand mixer or with a hand-held electric mixer, until smooth.

SERVE

Serve the cornbread straight out of the oven with the chipotle maple butter, scattering each serving with some crumbled tortilla chips.

FRIED CHICKEN WITH SMOKY BACON RANCH DIP

Fried chicken is one of those comforting and nostalgic foods that I find I crave more and more as I get older. A couple of years ago, fried chicken became trendy on the restaurant scene and, all of a sudden, this guilty pleasure was given a new lease on life. For Londoners, it was making a comeback, but having spent time in the U.S. and Asia, fried chicken never left the scene for me, and I still pine after some of the variations I have encountered over the years.

In order to make something truly special that would rival some of my best fried chicken memories, we use chicken "oysters," which we believe elevates our version to a higher league. Each oyster offers the perfect ratio of meat to skin that, once marinated, breaded and fried, results in a perfect, succulent, and crispy morsel of fried chicken.

We like to pimp them up for friends or at Christmas by serving them with sour cream, chives, and caviar.

INGREDIENTS

Serves 6

FOR THE BRINE:

½ cup/125 ml buttermilk
⅕ ounce/6 g salt
⅕ ounce/6 g coriander seeds, toasted and finely ground
⅒ ounce/3 g black peppercorns, toasted and finely ground

30 chicken oysters (alternatively, 1⅓ pounds/600 g boneless, skinless chicken thighs cut into quarters)

FOR THE RANCH DIP (you'll have more than you need—it keeps well for 3 to 4 days in the fridge, and is perfect in roast beef or chicken sandwiches or in a simple lettuce salad):

1¼ ounces/35 g shallots, thinly diced
1 clove garlic, crushed
¾ cup/200 g crème fraîche
7 tablespoons/100 ml buttermilk
¼ ounce/7 g dill, thinly chopped
¼ ounce/7 g chives, thinly snipped
Small pinch smoked paprika
½ tablespoon Korean chile paste
Small pinch freshly ground black pepper
Grated zest and juice of ¼ lime
⅓ teaspoon Maldon sea salt, finely ground

12 slices smoked bacon, diced

FOR THE FLOUR MIX:

¾ cup/100 g all-purpose flour
2 tablespoons semolina
2 teaspoons fine sea salt
⅕ ounce/6 g coriander seeds, toasted and ground (if you marinate the chicken for around 12 hours)
⅒ ounce/3 g black peppercorns, toasted and ground (if you marinate the chicken for around 12 hours)

½ cup/125 g unsalted butter
2 quarts/2 liters vegetable oil, for deep-frying
Lemon slices, to serve

CONTINUED

MAKE THE BRINE & MARINATE THE CHICKEN

Mix all the ingredients for the brine together in a bowl. Add the chicken oysters, cover, and chill for 12 to 24 hours.

MAKE THE RANCH DIP

Mix all the ingredients together, taste, and adjust the seasoning if necessary. Cover and chill until required.

COOK THE BACON

Line a baking sheet with parchment paper. Place the diced bacon in a frying pan, add just enough water to cover, and place over medium heat, stirring and skimming occasionally. After about 25 minutes, when all the water has evaporated, add the butter and keep stirring as the butter foams. When the bacon is dark and golden brown, strain it (you can keep the fat for using in other recipes), and pat the bacon bits with paper towels to remove excess butter and fat. Place the bacon bits on the baking sheet and put in an oven on the lowest setting for 30 minutes until dehydrated and crispy. Remove from the oven and set aside.

"WORK" THE CHICKEN

Wash the brine off the chicken and put the chicken in a large bowl. Add 6 tablespoons/90ml of cold water to the chicken pieces in the bowl, and squeeze them (almost kneading)—the water will be incorporated into the chicken and the fat from the skin will release and emulsify into the water. Add more water 1 to 2 tablespoons at a time, continuing to work the chicken, and after about 5 minutes the water coating the chicken will thicken and go creamy. This is super important, as it means the chicken will hold more flour, giving it a chunky, thick coating that will keep the chicken moist inside and crunchy on the outside—the thickness of the coating means the chicken won't dry out as it fries.

MAKE THE FLOUR MIX & FRY THE CHICKEN

Heat the vegetable oil in a deep-fat fryer or large, deep saucepan until it reaches 340°F/170°C. Mix all of the ingredients for the flour mix together in a bowl. Place the chicken pieces one by one (without draining the water off) in the flour mix and roll carefully until they're completely covered. Drop 6 to 10 pieces of chicken at a time (depending how big your fryer or saucepan is) into the hot oil and fry for 4 minutes. Remove carefully and leave to drain on paper towels.

SERVE

Serve the fried chicken with lemon slices and the ranch dip scattered with smoky bacon bits.

Gillardeau Rock
(FRANCE)

Duchy Native
(ENGL...

Lindisfarn...

BOBBY "BANJO" GROVES

Chief Oysterman

In Hollywood movies, you usually see oysters being
swallowed whole. This is not the best way to eat an oyster.
You should chew it a few times, really get the taste of it,
before swallowing. With English oysters, I suggest nothing
more than lemon juice as an accompaniment, but we also
offer mignonette and ponzu sauces.

I grew up in Maldon, famous for its sea salt. So I love East
Coast oysters—Maldon, West Mersea, Colchester—and
started shucking them when I was a teenager, out on the
Maldon Prom. I have some of these oysters on the cart
whenever I can. During the summer, you have to forget
about native oysters. They're put back to breed, and the
season is done. But we keep serving the Gillardeau, which
is the ultimate Fine de Claire. They don't go as milky in
the summer as others do, which makes them more popular.
Some people like that deeper, milky taste, though. It's
actually an oyster's form of reproductive fluid, but not
everyone wants to know that.

STARTERS

SWEET RED PRAWNS WITH BLOOD ORANGE, PISTACHIO, AND DILL

Sweet red prawns (Gambero Rosso) served raw, lightly marinated or cured, are really stunning, and guests at the Firehouse are falling in love with them. Long gone are the days of the boring shrimp cocktail with overcooked frozen shrimp from some distant sea. These days, restaurants in cities this side of the Atlantic and across the pond are serving these jewels in their freshest possible state, so that we can enjoy their true flavor.

This easy dish is so tasty—you just need to make sure you source the best possible ingredients. I hope you love it as much as I do.

INGREDIENTS

Serves 4

2 pounds/1 kg (20 to 24) raw shell-on fresh or frozen red prawns (Gambero Rosso) or other very large wild-caught shrimp
Superfine sugar
Maldon sea salt

1 blood orange or Sicilian orange
1 bunch dill
3 ounces/80 g green pistachios, shelled
4 tablespoons extra virgin olive oil

CURE THE PRAWNS

Peel and devein the prawns. Reserve the shells and heads for making prawn stock or oil, if you like.

Make a curing mix with a 60/40 ratio of sugar and salt, strips of orange zest and the dill stems. Add the prawns to the mixture and leave them at room temperature to cure for 20 minutes. Rinse, pat dry with paper towels, and set aside until ready to serve.

TOAST THE PISTACHIOS

Preheat the oven to 275°F/140°C. Spread the pistachios out on a baking sheet, transfer to the oven and bake for 6 to 7 minutes, or until crispy and fragrant. Remove from the oven and chop coarsely.

SERVE

Chill 4 plates. Place 5 or 6 prawns on each chilled plate. Spoon 1 tablespoon of olive oil onto each plate, then squeeze the juice of ¼ orange over each serving. Scatter the pistachios over the top or in little piles around the edges. Garnish with little dill fronds and sprinkle with salt. Very finely grate over a little orange zest and serve immediately.

SEA TROUT CRUDO WITH YELLOW MOLE AND CILANTRO

When we were creating the Firehouse menu, we based each section on a cooking station. One of my favorite sections of contemporary restaurants in New York or San Francisco is the raw or *crudo* section. Raw or cured seafood and fish is a great way to start a meal. You might find a traditional *fruits de mer* platter on offer, which is lovely, but I prefer a more unique approach, where you see the hand of the chef at work. This sea trout *crudo*, enhanced by cured fish roe, was the first dish from this section that we put on the menu. It is very fresh, sexy, refreshing, and tasty, and in my view captures perfectly the identity of Chiltern Firehouse.

This dish is pleasingly versatile, with the curing technique working well with many different fish: you could use salmon or red snapper, tuna, or even yellowtail in place of the sea trout. Thinly slice some fresh chiles and add them as a garnish if you like.

INGREDIENTS

Serves 4

FOR THE CILANTRO OIL:

7 ounces/200 g picked cilantro leaves
¾ cup/200 ml grapeseed oil
1 teaspoon Maldon sea salt

FOR THE YELLOW MOLE:

4 ounces/125 g peeled and chopped
  mango flesh
2½ ounces/75 g chopped pineapple
  flesh from the prepared pineapple
½ ounce/12 g grated fresh horseradish
1 tablespoon fish sauce
¼ teaspoon fresh red chile seeds
  or dried chile flakes
⅙ ounce/5 g cilantro stalks
5 tablespoons/70 ml lime juice
Pinch table salt, to taste

FOR THE CURED SALMON CAVIAR:

3½ ounces/100 g salmon caviar
  (also called roe)
2 teaspoons white soy sauce
1 tablespoon superfine sugar
¾ cup/200 ml dashi

1 (4⅓ pounds/2 kg) sea trout, gutted,
  cleaned, filleted, scaled, pin-boned
  (you can ask your fishmonger to do
  this), and cured (see page 106)
1 apple
½ lemon, for squeezing
1 pineapple, peeled, cored, finely
  diced, and set aside in its own juice
4 ounces/125 g cilantro, leaves picked

CONTINUED

MAKE THE CILANTRO OIL   Make the oil following the technique on page 183.

MAKE THE YELLOW MOLE   Place all the ingredients in a food processor or a blender and process to a smooth purée. Pass through a fine-mesh sieve into a bowl, cover, and chill until needed.

CURE THE SALMON CAVIAR   Remove the roe from the jar and rinse in a sieve under cold running water. Transfer to a bowl and add the soy sauce, sugar, and dashi. Chill for about 45 minutes, until the roe hardens and is nice and crunchy. Drain in a sieve and chill the caviar until ready to serve.

PREPARE THE SEA TROUT   Thinly slice the fish into ¼-inch/5-mm-thick pieces, allowing about 2½ ounces/70 g per portion.

PREPARE THE APPLE   Keeping the skin on, slice the apple into batons ⅛ inch/2.5 mm thick and ¾ inch/ 2 cm long. Sprinkle the batons with a little lemon juice to prevent them oxidizing.

SERVE   Chill 4 serving plates. Place 2 to 3 generous tablespoons of yellow mole on the bottom of each plate and place pieces of cured fish on top. Top each with about 1 ounce/30 g of the diced pineapple, 1 ounce/30 g of apple batons, and cilantro leaves. Spoon 1 tablespoon of cured roe on top and drizzle with cilantro oil. Serve cold.

CURED SEA BREAM, GREEN OLIVE PURÉE, AND FENNEL

Curing is one of my favorite ways to prepare sea bream. I remember when I was running Bacchus on Hoxton Street, east London, I was already working with seared or raw bream. The quality of sea bream here in the UK is really good, and it's reasonably priced and easy to source. It also has the advantage of being able to hold its own when paired with strong flavors, such as this green olive purée. If you cannot find bream, substitute sea bass or snapper.

If you prefer, briefly sear or blowtorch the fish skin before serving it. The charred flavor of the skin and the oiliness that it releases into the meat is superb.

INGREDIENTS

Serves 4

FOR THE SPINACH PURÉE:

About 3 ounces/80 to 90 g baby
  spinach leaves
Pinch salt, for blanching

FOR THE APPLE PURÉE:

2 Granny Smith apples
1 teaspoon superfine sugar
1 tablespoon freshly squeezed
  lemon juice
1 cup/250 ml water
Maldon sea salt, to taste

FOR THE GREEN OLIVE PURÉE:

2 ounces/60 g fennel
3½ ounces/100 g pitted Gordal
  or Cerignola olives
2⅓ ounces/70 g apple purée
1 ounce/30 g spinach purée
2 teaspoons extra virgin olive oil
1 teaspoon olive brine (from the can
  or jar of olives)
Maldon sea salt, to season

2 fillets farmed or wild sea bream
  (about 8½ ounces/250 g each), scaled
  pin-boned, and cured (see page 106)

FOR THE FENNEL:

2 fennel bulbs with fronds
Extra virgin olive oil, for drizzling
Maldon sea salt, to season
Freshly squeezed lemon juice,
  to season

TO SERVE:

Extra virgin olive oil
Freshly squeezed lemon juice
Maldon sea salt

CONTINUED

MAKE THE SPINACH PURÉE

Blanch the spinach for 30 seconds in a large saucepan of boiling, well salted water. Drain and refresh in a bowl of ice-cold water, then squeeze out the excess water over a bowl, reserving a small amount. Put the spinach in a blender and blend until smooth, then add the reserved spinach water and blend again until it forms a paste. You need the purée to have a neutral flavor, so resist seasoning it—the salt from the blanching water should be enough.

MAKE THE APPLE PURÉE

Peel the apples and cut them into small to medium dice—the smaller the dice, the quicker the apple will cook. Put the diced apples and remaining purée ingredients in a small saucepan with a lid. Cook, covered, for 15 to 20 minutes until the apple is soft. Blend with a stick blender until puréed and season with salt to taste, then let it cool.

MAKE THE GREEN OLIVE PURÉE

Thinly shave the fennel, season with salt, and place in a saucepan with a little water (just enough to cover the bottom of the pan). Cover, place over low heat, and cook for 8 to 10 minutes. Remove from the heat, drain, and set aside.

Bring a saucepan of water to a boil, add the pitted olives and boil for 10 minutes. Drain well. Place the drained olives and the remaining purée ingredients (including the cooked fennel and the apple and spinach purées) in a powerful blender and blend to a smooth purée. Pass it through a fine-mesh sieve into a clean squeeze bottle and chill until needed.

PREPARE THE FISH

Once the fish is cured, you can char the skin in a frying pan or with a blowtorch. If using a frying pan, brush the skin with a little grapeseed oil, heat a frying pan until very hot, and sear the fish very quickly, skin side down, for 30 seconds. If using a blowtorch, place the fish fillets skin side up on a wire rack with a drip tray underneath, making sure there is space between the fillets. Char the skin briefly with a blowtorch until fragrant.

Let the fish cool on a clean chopping board for 1 minute then gently peel off the skin to expose the fatty layer underneath. Cut into thin slices widthwise (leave the skin on, if you prefer). Keep the skin for serving, if you wish.

PREPARE THE FENNEL

While the fish is curing, thinly shave the fennel bulbs, retaining the fronds to garnish. Place the shaved fennel in a bowl, drizzle with olive oil, and season with salt and lemon juice. Set aside for 30 minutes before serving.

SERVE

Spoon or pipe 2 tablespoons of the green olive purée onto each plate, place slices of the fish around the purée, and garnish generously with fennel shavings. Drizzle with olive oil and season with lemon juice. Sprinkle with sea salt and finish with fennel fronds.

HOW WE CURE OUR FISH

Curing fish preserves the natural sweetness of the flesh, and the salt tightens the protein strands to keep the fillet nice and firm. We cure fish with a mixture of sugar and salt (using a ratio of 60 percent superfine sugar to 40 percent fine sea salt), sometimes adding spices and herbs. Most of our crudos or raw fish dishes use this technique (see pages 96, 98, and 102).

Make sure your fillets are pin-boned and scaled.

Combine the sugar and salt thoroughly before curing the fish. Cover the bottom of a tray with some of the sugar and salt mix. Place the fillets flesh side down in the sugar and salt mixture, then cover the fillet completely with the rest of the mixture. Let it sit at room temperature for 45 to 90 minutes, depending on the size of the fish.

Wash the cure off the fish under cold running water, then pat it dry with kitchen towels. Set it aside ready for portioning.

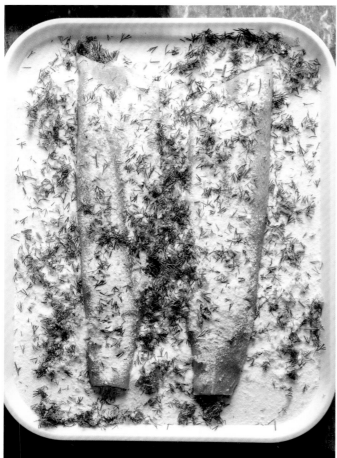

SCALLOP CRUDO WITH YOUNG TURNIPS AND TIGER'S MILK

I am amazed at the quality of scallops here in the UK; they are so firm and sweet in the winter months that they are best served raw. In this quick dish, we used the roe to make a punchy dressing similar to *leche de tigre*, or tiger's milk (usually made with seasoned fish trimmings, fresh chile, and lime juice—the acid "eats" the protein and produces a milky liquid), which is a starting ingredient of a good ceviche. Inspired by a recent trip to Peru, I start the tiger's milk with the usual ingredients, then add scallop roe to make the dish complex and rich, while retaining the sweetness of the scallops.

I urge you to try different variations of this dish, such as serving the scallops with a handful of edamame, roughly diced grapefruit segments, a small bunch of chopped basil, and a dressing made of low-salt soy sauce, grapefruit juice, and olive oil.

INGREDIENTS

Serves 6

12 baby turnips, tops cleaned, and small soft leaves retained for garnish
1 tablespoon salt
6 live sea scallops in their shells

FOR THE SCALLOP ROE TIGER'S MILK:

2½ ounces/75 g scallop roe, washed (from 6 scallops)
1 small clove garlic, crushed
2 red chiles, seeded
½ tablespoon freshly squeezed lemon juice

1/10 ounce/3 g cilantro
1 tablespoon chipotle paste
1 free-range egg yolk
2 tablespoons buttermilk
½ teaspoon instant dashi

1 large turnip, thinly sliced (preferably on a mandoline) and cut into 1¼-inch/3-cm rounds with a cutter
1 small bunch sea purslane, leaves picked (or tender samphire tops)
20 pieces of stonecrop or samphire
Extra virgin olive oil, for drizzling

PREPARE THE BABY TURNIPS

Quarter the baby turnips, soak in lightly salted water for 20 to 30 minutes, drain, and set aside.

CLEAN THE SCALLOPS

Dissolve the salt in 1 quart/1 liter of water. Shuck the scallops, being careful not to damage the meat. Gently remove the muscle from the skirt and roe. Rinse the scallop meat in the salted water to remove any membrane or grit and pat dry with paper towels. Place in a clean container and chill until ready to serve. Remove the roe from the skirt, wash them in the salted water and pat them dry.

MAKE THE SCALLOP ROE TIGER'S MILK

Place all the ingredients in a blender or the bowl of a food processor and blend to form a smooth paste. Pass the paste through a fine-mesh sieve into a clean bowl, cover, and chill until needed.

SERVE

Chill 6 plates. Spoon the tiger's milk onto each plate to make a pool of sauce. Cut each scallop into 6 pieces. Arrange baby turnip quarters and round slices around the scallops. Place the herbs on top of the turnips and scallop and drizzle with olive oil.

STEAK TARTARE

Steak tartare is a classic dish that can be found in restaurants all over North America. For it to be at its best, it must be made with very good-quality beef. At the Firehouse, we use beef filet tails left over from our main-course filet steak and—unlike many versions—we briefly sear the meat before cutting it, which adds another layer of flavor and texture. We use classic garnishes to dress our tartare but also add our own chipotle sauce and pine nut emulsion and serve Firehouse sauce on the side.

INGREDIENTS

Serves 4

FOR THE PINE NUT EMULSION:

1 ounce/30 g pine nuts
1 free-range egg yolk
2½ tablespoons whole milk
¼ teaspoon xanthan gum
½ teaspoon salt
3½ tablespoons grapeseed oil

FOR THE FIREHOUSE SAUCE:

2 tablespoons grapeseed oil
17 ounces/500 g cored Granny Smith apples, diced
10 ounces/300 g onions, diced
1⅓ ounces/40 g garlic cloves
10 ounces/300 g red chiles, half cut lengthwise and seeded, half left whole and coarsely chopped
2 drops liquid hickory smoke (or to taste)
¾ cup/180 ml red wine vinegar
¾ cup/180 ml water
⅜ cup/125 g superfine sugar
Maldon sea salt, to taste

CONTINUED

14 ounces/400 g beef filet tips or filet steak (order the tips from your butcher), cut into 4 pieces and chilled
Extra virgin olive oil, for brushing
4 ounces/125 g dense, crusty white bread (4 slices)
8 cornichons, thinly chopped
4 teaspoons thinly chopped shallot
12 breakfast radishes, finely chopped
4 sprigs flat-leaf parsley, finely sliced
8 anchovy fillets in oil, chopped
4 teaspoons chipotle sauce, or more to taste
Tabasco
4 good-quality, free-range egg yolks, at room temperature
Maldon sea salt and freshly ground black pepper

MAKE THE PINE NUT EMULSION

Preheat the oven to 325°F/160°C. Place the pine nuts on a baking sheet and bake for 8 to 12 minutes, until golden. Place a food processor with the egg yolk, milk, xanthan gum, and salt and blend to a fine purée. Slowly drizzle the grapeseed oil into the mixture while the motor is still running, to form an emulsion. Pass through a fine-mesh sieve into a jar, then transfer to a squeeze bottle and chill until required.

MAKE THE FIREHOUSE SAUCE

At the Firehouse, we smoke the apple, onion, garlic, and chile in a smoker for 2 hours. If you don't have a smoker, add a few drops of liquid smoke after you've made the sauce.

Heat the grapeseed oil in a large saucepan over medium-low heat. Add the smoked or unsmoked apple, onion, garlic, and chile and cook for about 45 minutes, until dark and soft. Add the red wine vinegar, water, and sugar, season with salt to taste, cover, and cook for 1 hour over low heat. Transfer the mixture to the bowl of a food processor or a blender and blend until smooth, then pass through a fine-mesh sieve into a bowl, and cover and chill overnight. The next day, add a little cold water if it's too thick and pasty, and reseason to taste. It will keep in the fridge for 2 weeks.

SEAR THE STEAK

Brush the chilled steaks with a little oil and season with salt. Heat a nonstick frying pan over high heat until very hot, then sear the steaks one at a time for about 15 seconds on each side, until brown and lightly caramelized. Remove from the heat, transfer to a cool plate and leave somewhere cool or transfer immediately to the fridge to stop the cooking process. Once cool, chop the meat into small dice, season to taste with salt and pepper, mix, then divide into 4 equal portions.

SERVE

Toast the bread slices and cut them in half. Place a steak patty in a bowl and arrange chopped cornichon, shallot, radish, parsley, and anchovies around the plate, with toast on the side. Add 1 teaspoon of chipotle sauce and 1 tablespoon of the pine nut emulsion to the bowl, then add 3 drops of Tabasco, taste, and adjust seasoning with sea salt and freshly ground black pepper. If you like the tartare spicier, add more chipotle sauce; if you like it more creamy, add more pine nut emulsion. Repeat with the remaining 3 servings, adding an egg yolk to each serving. Serve the Firehouse sauce on the side.

FIREHOUSE CAESAR

At some point in my career, I took what Bugs Bunny called "the wrong turn in Albuquerque" and ended up in Santa Fe, New Mexico, for a year and a half. At first I was apprehensive about moving from New York to this small city with my dog, cat, and girlfriend in tow. New Mexico is incredibly beautiful, but it was a hard place to live in, particularly at the end of 2001 when America was going through a very difficult time.

Unfortunately many of my memories are sad: the cat died, the dog stayed when I returned to New York (very hard decision!), and my girlfriend and I broke up. But I did meet and become good friends with a chef, Mark Miller, who inspired me more than most in my career. He taught me about real Mexican cuisine, how to make a good Caesar salad, and how to work with chiles. And he told me about a restaurant in Catalonia run by a very talented chef by the name of Ferran. Somehow I secured an internship there, so in 2003 I was off and away. I hold many dear memories from New Mexico and can still make a nice Caesar salad, thanks to you, MM! My version includes crispy chicken skin and emulsion to add crunch and a creamy texture.

INGREDIENTS

Serves 4 as a main course
or 4 to 6 as a starter

FOR THE BREAD TUILES:

1 loaf day-old country or sourdough
  bread
Extra virgin olive oil, for brushing
Salt and pepper

FOR THE CAESAR DRESSING:

1½ cloves garlic, very thinly sliced with
  a Microplane or a small, sharp knife
5 fillets Ortiz anchovies, or other brand
  of good-quality anchovy fillets in oil
2 free-range egg yolks
3½ tablespoons red wine vinegar
2 teaspoons Dijon mustard
1 cup/250 ml grapeseed oil
2½ ounces/75 g Parmesan cheese,
  thinly sliced with a Microplane
  or mandoline
Juice of ½ lemon
½ teaspoon Worcestershire sauce
2 drops Tabasco
Pinch table salt
Freshly ground black pepper

FOR THE CRISPY CHICKEN SKIN:

Skin from 1 whole free-range chicken
  (ask your butcher, or buy 4 chicken
  breasts with the skin on, remove the
  skin, and freeze the breasts to use
  another time)

FOR THE LETTUCE EMULSION:

8 ounces/240 g Little Gem lettuce,
  green leaves only
Table salt
1½ teaspoons Dijon mustard
¾ cup/200 ml grapeseed oil
7 tablespoons/100 ml cold water

4 romaine lettuce hearts, cut into
  bite-sized pieces
7 ounces/200 g Parmesan cheese,
  sliced into fine shavings
8 fillets anchovies, halved lengthwise
  (use Ortiz or another brand of good-
  quality anchovy fillets in oil)

CONTINUED

MAKE THE BREAD TUILES

Preheat the oven to 325°F/160°C. Cut 8 to 12 very thin slices of bread from the loaf so you have 2 slices per person. Place on a baking sheet, brush with extra virgin olive oil on both sides, and season with salt and pepper. Bake for 15 to 20 minutes until golden and crispy, then remove from the oven, break into bite-sized pieces, and set aside. Keep the oven on.

MAKE THE CAESAR DRESSING

Place the garlic, anchovies, egg yolks, red wine vinegar, and mustard in a blender or a food processor and blend until smooth. While the motor is still running, slowly drizzle in the grapeseed oil to create an emulsion. Transfer the dressing to a bowl, whisk in the remaining ingredients, check the seasoning, and set aside.

MAKE THE CRISPY CHICKEN SKINS

Line a baking sheet with parchment paper. Scrape the excess fat from the chicken skin. Place the skin on the parchment, laying it flat over the whole tray in two layers. Place another piece of parchment paper on top, with another baking sheet on top of that. Bake for 30 to 40 minutes until golden and crisp, then remove from the oven, remove the top tray and parchment from the skin, and set aside.

MAKE THE LETTUCE EMULSION

Blanch the lettuce leaves in a saucepan of boiling salted water for 2 seconds, then refresh in a bowl of ice-cold water. Drain well, patting off any excess water with paper towels.

Place the lettuce, a pinch of salt, and the mustard in the bowl of a food processor and blend at high speed until it forms a smooth purée, then reduce the speed and slowly drizzle in the oil and water, a little of each at a time, to create an emulsion. Pass through a fine-mesh sieve into a clean bowl and set aside.

SERVE

Toss the romaine lettuce in the Caesar dressing until the leaves are evenly covered. Spoon a small amount of the lettuce emulsion into the bottom of 4 to 6 serving bowls, enough to cover the bottom of each. Then layer up the dressed leaves, Parmesan shavings, bread tuiles, crispy chicken skin, and anchovies so that they are well distributed through the salad. Finish with another layer of all the elements over the top.

TENDER LEAVES AND BEETS WITH CANDIED PECANS

A salad can be just a salad, or it can be something truly magnificent. To make a salad magnificent, follow these rules:

- Use the best possible cultivated greens from a local vegetable supplier and a mix of different lettuces with a variety of flavors and textures (soft, crunchy, bitter, spicy).

- Use a mix of soft herbs such as chervil, chives, tarragon, basil, dill, parsley, and cilantro.

- Use roasted and raw vegetables, thinly sliced or cut into chunks.

- Use fruits that will add sweetness, acidity, and crunch.

- Sprinkle the salad with caramelized, roasted, or candied dried fruits.

- Keep the dressing simple, but make sure it is well seasoned (I like using soy sauce or fish sauce), and use a good-quality sherry, red wine, balsamic, cider, or champagne vinegar or freshly squeezed citrus juice (lemon, lime, grapefruit, or orange). Use high-quality raw (virgin) oils such as extra virgin olive oil, canola oil, or grapeseed oil.

- Dress your salad just before serving, tossing the ingredients with the dressing in a very large bowl until every little bit of salad is lightly coated (don't use an excessive amount of dressing).

INGREDIENTS

Serves 4

FOR THE ROASTED BEETS:

16 purple beets, washed
4 sprigs thyme
1 bay leaf
3 pinches Maldon sea salt,
  plus extra to season
3 tablespoons extra virgin olive oil,
  plus extra for drizzling

FOR THE CANDIED PECANS

1 cup/250 ml water
1¼ cups/250 g superfine sugar
4 ounces/125 g pecans
2 cups/500 ml grapeseed oil,
  for deep-frying
Maldon sea salt, for sprinkling

FOR THE HOUSE DRESSING

2 tablespoons white soy sauce
  or light soy sauce
2 tablespoons sherry vinegar
4 tablespoons extra virgin olive oil
Maldon sea salt and freshly ground
  black pepper

FOR THE SALAD:

1 ounce/30 g Baby Candy beets
1 ounce/30 g breakfast radishes
14 ounces/400 g mixed salad leaves
  (2 generous handfuls per person);
  we use 1 Castelfranco lettuce and
  1 oak lettuce or Lollo Rosso
Fresh herbs and wild leaves; we use
  3½ ounces/100 g each wild arugula,
  mizuna, and wild watercress tops, plus
  nasturtium leaves, purslane, sorrel,
  tender beet tops, radish tops, dill,
  chervil, or any other soft herbs
3 oranges, peeled and segmented,
  then stored in juice squeezed from
  trimmings
Maldon sea salt, to season

CONTINUED

ROAST THE BEETROOT

Preheat the oven to 325°F/160°C. Line a roasting tray with foil. Place the purple beets on the lined tray with the thyme, bay leaf, salt, and olive oil, toss, then cover with another piece of foil and seal the edges to create a sealed pouch so the beets roast and steam at the same time. Cook in the oven for 30 to 40 minutes, until cooked through—the foil package should puff up slightly if you have sealed it properly. Remove from the oven and take the beets out of the foil package. Leave until they're cool enough to handle, then peel. The skins should rub off easily with a piece of paper towel (wear gloves to avoid staining your hands). Cut the peeled beets into quarters, place in a bowl, and dress lightly in olive oil and salt. If using that day, keep at room temperature, but if making a day ahead, cover and store in the fridge.

MAKE THE CANDIED PECANS

Place the water and sugar in a saucepan and bring to a boil. Simmer for 3 minutes, until the sugar has dissolved. Stir in the nuts to coat them in the sugar syrup and continue to cook for a further 5 minutes, stirring occasionally, until dark golden brown. Strain off the syrup, transfer the nuts to a wire rack sitting over a tray or paper towel to catch the drips, and leave to dry. This gives them an even coating of sugar so that when they are fried they will color evenly. Once cool, heat the oil in a deep saucepan or deep-fat fryer until it reaches 320°F/160°C. Fry the nuts in batches for 1½ to 2 minutes, until golden in color and caramelized. They will bubble a lot at first. Once the bubbling subsides, remove them with a slotted spoon, place them back on the wire rack and season lightly with Maldon salt.

MAKE THE HOUSE DRESSING

Combine all the ingredients and mix lightly with a fork (no need to whisk or emulsify), then set aside.

PREPARE THE BABY BEETS & RADISHES

Scrape the baby beets and radishes clean around the stems then wash them. Slice as thinly as possible (we use a mandoline) and store in cold water to keep them crisp and fresh until ready to serve.

ASSEMBLE & SERVE

Put a small amount (about 1½ tablespoons) of the dressing in a large mixing bowl, swirl it around, then gently drop in the salad leaves and toss. There should be no dressing in the bottom of the bowl and the leaves should be lightly coated and glossy, not overdressed and soggy. Arrange some of the larger leaves in 4 individual serving dishes, then scatter over roasted beets, candied pecans, herbs, sliced raw beets and radishes and orange segments. Add another layer of larger leaves and then more garnishes again, using a light touch so the salad looks light and fresh. Season with salt to taste.

ROMAIN AUDRERIE

Head Sommelier

I grew up in Limousin, a rural part of France, and moved to Paris to do a master's degree in advertising. I spent five years at the Sorbonne immersed in marketing, brand identity, and semiology.

Wine is pleasure! My parents were quite nerdy about food, but they were not passionate about wine. This was my personal discovery.

A Château Citran from Haut-Médoc was my first insight into the depth and complexity of wine. Then an Australian chardonnay. I had been drinking white wine in France without even knowing it was chardonnay. How embarrassing! But we have to start somewhere.

California and Oregon now account for about 10 percent of our sales, which is very high for London. Every sommelier's nightmare is a table that you secretly know would prefer to be drinking Red Bull and Coke. The pleasure of the Firehouse is the level of interest our guests have in exploring wines. And I am always happy to introduce one of our back-vintage Diamond Creeks. We are all fanatics for Diamond Creek.

LAST SUPPER

A Riesling Singerriedel from the Wachau. I drank it in Austria in 2010 and it brought me to tears. It just changed my life.

LOBSTER XO NOODLES

During my travels in Asia, and through exploring large Chinese communities in cities I've lived in, I have developed a huge passion for lobster XO noodles, and this is our interpretation. A great version of this dish is unfortunately becoming harder to find. Cooking the lobster correctly is crucial, but so also is finding or making the right noodle and developing a fantastic XO paste. I like to eat it with the lobster off the shell.

The XO paste can be made well in advance, and there will be some left over to use in other dishes. It keeps for months in the fridge, and complements steamed or grilled fish or seafood perfectly. In fact, it's great with almost anything.

If you can't find dried scallops or dried shrimp (for the XO paste), dry your own by spreading 5 ounces/150 g fresh shelled shrimp and 3¾ ounces/110 g fresh scallops on separate baking sheets and drying them in the oven on its lowest setting (1 to 2 hours for shrimp, 3 hours for scallops).

INGREDIENTS

Serves 4

FOR THE XO PASTE:
1¼ ounces/35 g dried scallops
2 ounces/65 g dried shelled shrimp
⅓ ounce/10 g shrimp paste
1½ cups/350 ml grapeseed oil
3½ ounces/100 g shallots, thinly sliced
3½ ounces/100 g garlic cloves, thinly sliced
¾ ounce/20 g dried small red chiles, rehydrated and cut into thin strips
1¼ ounces/35 g fresh long red chile, seeded and cut into thin strips
2 ounces/65 g scraps smoked ham, thinly sliced
4 teaspoons superfine sugar
1½ tablespoons scallop water (reserved from rehydrating the scallops)

8 ounces/240 g raw, peeled lobster tail
7 ounces/200 g cherry tomatoes
1 tablespoon extra virgin olive oil
1¼ cups/300 ml grapeseed oil
5 shallots, thinly sliced lengthwise
4 cloves garlic, thinly sliced lengthwise
9 ounces/250 g De Cecco (or similar brand) egg noodles
Juice of 2 lemons, to season
Light soy sauce, to season
Maldon sea salt
4 shiso leaves, torn, to garnish

REHYDRATE THE DRIED SCALLOPS & SHRIMP

Place the dried scallops and shrimp in warm water and leave them to soak for a few hours until they plump up a little. Reserve the soaking liquid.

MAKE THE XO PASTE

Preheat the oven to 225°F/110°C. Line a baking sheet with parchment paper and spread the shrimp paste on the paper. Bake for 1 hour until soft, then remove from the oven and set aside.

Meanwhile, heat the oil in a deep saucepan, add the shallots and garlic, and fry gently for about 10 minutes, until golden. Remove from the heat and drain the shallots and garlic, returning the oil to the pan. Heat the oil again over medium heat, until it reaches 355°F/180°C. Add the rehydrated and fresh chiles and fry for 10 to 15 minutes, until golden and crisp—the bubbles will subside and there will be a caramelized smell.

CONTINUED

Remove the chiles with a slotted spoon and drain on paper towels. Add the ham to the oil and fry for 5 minutes until golden, then add the shellfish to the pan with the ham and fry for about 8 minutes, until golden. Add the baked shrimp paste and sugar to the pan, stir, and caramelize, letting the sugar dissolve, then add the scallop water and cook for 10 minutes, until the water evaporates, leaving a paste. Remove from the heat and leave to cool.

Blend all the ingredients together in a powerful blender or a food processor until they reach the consistency of thick cream. Store in a sealed container until required.

CURE THE LOBSTER

Cure the lobster according to the technique on page 106, then rinse, pat dry, and cut into medium bite-sized chunks.

BAKE THE TOMATOES

Preheat the oven to 300°F/150°C and line a baking sheet with parchment paper. Cut the tomatoes in half lengthwise, place cut side up in a single layer on the lined baking sheet, and drizzle with the olive oil, then season and bake for 2 hours, until they resemble sun-dried tomatoes. Remove from the oven and set aside.

FRY THE SHALLOTS & GARLIC

Heat the grapeseed oil in a deep saucepan until it reaches 285°F/140°C. Fry the shallots for 3 to 4 minutes, until crispy, then remove with a slotted spoon and drain on paper towels. Repeat with the garlic, frying it for 2 to 3 minutes, until crispy but not burnt, then drain on paper towels. Set aside until ready to serve.

BLANCH THE NOODLES AND MAKE THE SAUCE

You will need two big pans: one for blanching the noodles and one for cooking the sauce.

Fill one pan with water and bring to a boil. Add the noodles and blanch for about 1 minute, then drain, retaining the cooking water.

To make the sauce, place the second pan over medium heat, then add a generous 8 tablespoons/120 ml of the XO paste. Fry for about 2 minutes, until fragrant. Add the tomatoes, then add the blanched noodles. The sauce will have split, so start stirring in some of the noodle cooking water, a small ladle at a time, and when the pasta is almost cooked (it should take about 2 minutes), season the sauce to taste with salt, lemon juice, and a little light soy sauce. Reduce the heat under the saucepan with the noodles and add the lobster. Cook, stirring, for 1 minute, then remove from the heat and keep stirring. Check the seasoning.

SERVE

Warm 4 bowls. Divide the lobster and noodles between the bowls, scatter with the fried shallot, garlic, and torn shiso leaves, and serve.

GREEN AND WHITE ASPARAGUS WITH BROWN BUTTER MAYONNAISE

The arrival of asparagus in spring is celebrated every year by chefs, and guests wait patiently for the short season to begin. If you are a lover of this beautiful ingredient, you try to eat as much as you can, so that you can bear another eleven months' wait.

Large asparagus is perfect for this dish, and I strongly recommend only making it when it's in season. Our dish is a twist on the classic asparagus and hollandaise; instead of hollandaise we opt for a rich and nutty brown butter mayonnaise. You can serve the asparagus with flakes of a special aged Gruyère or Parmesan cheese, too—it will be amazing!

INGREDIENTS

Serves 4 as a starter, or 2 as a light main

FOR THE BROWN BUTTER MAYONNAISE:

1⅔ cups/375 g unsalted butter, diced
4 free-range egg yolks
Juice of 1 lemon
Maldon sea salt

12 large spears green asparagus, washed, purple leaves removed from stems, and dried
4 large spears white asparagus, washed
Extra virgin olive oil, for grilling
Maldon sea salt
10 sprigs sweet woodruff or chervil, leaves picked
12 asparagus pea flowers or pea shoots

MAKE THE BROWN BUTTER MAYONNAISE

Warm a saucepan over medium heat and drop in the diced butter. Once it melts and begins to foam, whisk it continuously for 8 to 10 minutes, keeping the heat constant, until it becomes nutty and fragrant. The foam will die down a bit, then you will see the color change and the butter solids turn a toasted brown color. Remove from the heat and transfer to a metal jug (it will be very hot), and keep stirring for a minute to prevent the butter burning (it will keep cooking off the heat).

Add the yolks to the bowl of a food processor and add half the lemon juice. Blend for about 1 minute, until the yolks turn slightly pale, then slowly drizzle in the still-warm butter to make a mayonnaise. If it appears to be getting too thick, add a few drops of cold water to thin it out. Make sure you add all the butter, including the solids at the bottom (they are the best bit!). Season the mayonnaise with the remaining lemon juice and salt to taste.

GRILL THE ASPARAGUS

Heat a ridged grill pan. Dress the asparagus spears in olive oil and salt and grill them on each side until they are just tender when pressed with a metal skewer, then transfer to a tray and keep somewhere warm until ready to serve.

SERVE

Warm 4 plates. Spread a tablespoon of brown butter mayonnaise onto each plate and arrange the asparagus in a little pile, stacking them up slightly. Scatter with the herbs and flowers.

HERB GNOCCHI

Despite the fact that gnocchi are Italian, my love for these crispy, creamy, and herby morsels started in 1996 in San Francisco, California, while working in the kitchen of chef Wolfgang Puck's restaurant Postrio. I felt I was still at culinary school because I learned so much every day, and one of the skills I picked up was how to make gnocchi: I worked the pasta station for around eight months, so used to make them every day. The garnishes and the herbs changed, but the technique stayed the same and they are still amazing. Thank you, Mr. Puck!

INGREDIENTS

Serves 4

FOR THE PARMESAN CREAM:

¾ cup/200 g crème fraîche
3½ ounces/100 g Parmesan cheese, grated
2 tablespoons freshly squeezed lemon juice
Grated zest of 1 unwaxed lemon
Freshly ground black pepper
Few drops liquid smoke (to taste)

1 ounce/30 g morels or wild mushrooms (if morels are not in season), carefully brushed to remove dirt and halved lengthwise

FOR THE GNOCCHI:

9 ounces/250 g floury potatoes, peeled
2⅔ ounces/80 g 00 flour, plus extra to dust
1⅓ ounces/40 g Parmesan cheese, grated

½ ounce/15 g combination of flat-leaf parsley, chives, tarragon, and chervil, thinly chopped
Grated zest of ½ unwaxed lemon
4 teaspoons extra virgin olive oil, plus extra for drizzling
1½ to 2 free-range egg yolks
Maldon sea salt and freshly ground black pepper

3 tablespoons unsalted butter, for frying
1⅓ ounces/40 g fresh peas, freshly shucked and lightly blanched
1 tablespoon finely snipped chives
1 tablespoon finely chopped chervil
1 tablespoon finely chopped flat-leaf parsley
Maldon sea salt and lemon juice, to season
Freshly shaved pecorino or Parmesan cheese, to serve
2 handfuls arugula leaves, to serve
Olive oil, to serve
Lemon juice, to serve
Pea and arugula flowers, to serve

MAKE THE PARMESAN CREAM

Combine all the ingredients, season to taste, and set aside until ready to serve.

PREPARE THE MORELS

Line a baking sheet with paper towels. Plunge the morels into a bowl of cold water for a few seconds, moving them gently so as not to damage them, then remove them and lay them out on the lined tray. Discard the water and fill the bowl with fresh cold water, immerse the morels again, then remove and place on fresh sheets of paper towels.

CONTINUED

COOK THE POTATOES

Place the potatoes in a saucepan and cover with cold water. Bring to a simmer and cook over a low heat for 20 to 30 minutes, until they are cooked through.

PREPARE FOR MAKING THE GNOCCHI

While the potatoes are cooking, measure out the remaining gnocchi ingredients and clean a generous area of work surface for rolling the gnocchi. Put a second pan of water on to boil—this will be used to blanch the gnocchi. Dust a large baking sheet lightly with flour or line with parchment paper—this is what you will place the cooked gnocchi on.

MAKE THE GNOCCHI

When the potatoes are fully cooked, drain and allow to steam in the colander for a few minutes to cool and dry slightly. Put the potatoes through a ricer (if you have one), or mash them well, then spread out the mashed potatoes on a clean work surface. Scatter the remaining ingredients over the potatoes, popping the egg yolks in a well within the mixture so they don't spill out.

Gently knead the mixture to form a smooth dough, being sure to incorporate everything evenly but not working the dough too hard. Divide the dough into a few pieces and roll each piece into a log about ½ inch/1 cm in diameter. Using a thin, sharp knife, cut the logs into 48 to 60 small dumplings and sprinkle them with flour. Transfer the dumplings (using a bench scraper card if you have one) to the lined or floured tray as you cut them.

BLANCH THE GNOCCHI

Once the gnocchi are prepared and the second pan of water is boiling, prepare a bowl of ice-cold water and have a slotted spoon at hand. Lightly season the boiling water and blanch the gnocchi in batches for about 2 minutes, or until they float up to the surface. Transfer the gnocchi straight to the ice-cold water to cool for 2 to 3 minutes, then drain and lightly dress in the oil. Keep to one side until ready to fry (they can be made and blanched up to a day ahead, kept in the fridge in a sealed container).

FRY THE GNOCCHI & THE MORELS

Heat the 3 tablespoons of butter in a nonstick frying pan over medium heat and fry the gnocchi in batches for 4 to 5 minutes each side until golden on both sides. Once golden, transfer the gnocchi into a colander set over a saucepan or bowl (to strain off the butter). Fry the next batch, then transfer to the colander. Repeat until all the gnocchi are done.

Transfer the strained butter to the frying pan, place over medium heat and fry the morels for about 5 minutes. Add a little salt to draw out some of the liquid from the mushrooms, then return the gnocchi to the pan. Remove from the heat, add the peas, then the herbs, and season with salt and lemon juice to taste.

SERVE

Warm 4 bowls. When the gnocchi are warmed through and lightly glazed with the butter, transfer them to a clean tray. Spread 1¾ ounces/50 g of the Parmesan cream in a circle in each bowl and arrange the gnocchi around the cream, with the peas and morels. Scatter with shavings of pecorino or Parmesan, dress the arugula in olive oil and lemon juice and place over the gnocchi. Finish with pea and arugula flowers and serve immediately.

JERSEY ROYALS, WILD GARLIC, AND SLOW-COOKED EGG

This delicate dish is a simple seasonal starter that we put on the menu in our first spring at the Firehouse. Come springtime in the UK, nature blesses us with pungent flowering wild garlic, tiny Jersey Royal potatoes, and earthy morel mushrooms. These ingredients, served at their best, go hand in hand together, and it does not take much to make this into something very special. Jersey Royals grow only on the island of Jersey; if you cannot source them, use tiny new potatoes.

INGREDIENTS	Serves 6

FOR THE WILD GARLIC MAYONNAISE:

4 ounces/125 g wild garlic leaves (chives or the green part of green onions are both good alternatives if wild garlic is not available)
2 free-range egg yolks
1 tablespoon fish sauce
½ teaspoon Maldon sea salt
Juice of 2 limes
⅔ cup/160 ml grapeseed oil

36 small Jersey Royal potatoes or other small new potatoes, scrubbed
8 large free-range eggs, at room temperature
18 large morels or wild mushrooms (if morels are not in season), carefully brushed to remove dirt and halved lengthwise
2 tablespoons unsalted butter, for frying
Maldon sea salt, to taste
Wild garlic leaves and flowers, to garnish
Good quality olive oil, for drizzling

MAKE THE WILD GARLIC MAYONNAISE

Bring a large saucepan of water to a rapid boil and prepare a bowl of ice-cold water. Blanch the wild garlic leaves for 10 seconds, then remove them and plunge them into the ice-cold water, stirring to cool them quickly. Pick out the ice and pass the water and leaves through a sieve, squeezing any excess moisture out of the leaves. Place the egg yolks, blanched wild garlic leaves, fish sauce, salt, and half the lime juice in a blender or the bowl of a food processor. Blend until very smooth, then gradually add the oil until it is all incorporated and you have a smooth emulsion. Pass through a fine-mesh sieve into a bowl, taste, and adjust the seasoning with more lime juice and salt if necessary. If you want a spicier mayonnaise, blend in one or two raw wild garlic leaves. Transfer the mayonnaise to a squeeze bottle and set aside.

COOK THE POTATOES

Place the potatoes in a large saucepan and fill with water about 2 inches/5 cm above the potatoes. Add salt to the water and bring to a simmer over medium heat. Cook for about 35 minutes until tender (test them with a skewer) and, once cooked, drain and spread onto a tray lined with a clean, dry kitchen towel to draw out excess moisture. Set aside.

COOK THE EGGS

Poach the eggs according to the technique on page 137 (we list 8 eggs, to allow for any that don't poach quite as you'd like them, or whose yolks break). Remove and set aside until ready to serve.

CONTINUED

PREPARE THE MUSHROOMS	Line a baking sheet with paper towels. Plunge the mushrooms into a bowl of cold water for a few seconds, moving them gently so as not to damage them, then remove them and lay them out on the lined tray. Discard the water and fill the bowl with fresh cold water, immerse the morels again, then remove and place on fresh paper towels.
COOK THE MUSHROOMS	Warm 6 serving plates. Melt the butter in a large frying pan or saucepan over low heat. Add the morels and sauté gently for 3 to 4 minutes, adding a little salt, until almost cooked through. Just before they are ready, add 2 tablespoons of water and swirl it in the pan to emulsify it with the butter, scraping up any bits that are stuck to the pan. Add the cooked potatoes and 3 wild garlic leaves per plate. Check for seasoning, remove from the heat and keep warm.
SERVE	Squeeze 6 small dollops of wild garlic mayonnaise onto each plate and place a potato on each one (these will hold the egg in place). Place a poached egg in the middle of each plate then place the morels around the potatoes and drape the wilted wild garlic leaves over. Dress the egg with any juices from the pan you cooked the mushrooms in, and scatter with garlic flowers. Drizzle with olive oil and serve immediately.

HOW TO POACH AN EGG, CHEF-STYLE

Firstly, you need the deepest pan you have (such as one you cook spaghetti in).

For each quart/liter of water add 6 tablespoons/90 ml vinegar (white wine or apple cider vinegar) and a pinch of salt.

Fill the pot almost to the brim with water and bring it to a boil. While you are waiting for the water to come to a boil, get your eggs ready by breaking them into individual ramekins, teacups, or small bowls.

Once the water is boiling, mix it gently to form a whirlpool in the center. Drop each egg into the water, as close to the edge of the pan as possible (not the middle). It will then be pulled down into the middle of the whirlpool and, the bigger your pan, the longer it will take for it to be drawn into the middle and the better shape it will have.

Your first egg will always go wrong. Remove and discard it. The dregs of egg white left in the pan will actually make the water better to poach in.

Cook each egg in the water for 3 minutes, remove with a slotted spoon and place on a napkin or paper towels to absorb the water, then serve.

BARLEY AND OAT RISOTTO WITH ZUCCHINI, ARTICHOKES, SPINACH, AND HERBS

This dish is the perfect platform to showcase vegetables at their best. I like to eat it in a bowl so that the fresh cream can be pulled in around the oats and you can enjoy a little bit of it in every spoonful.

INGREDIENTS	Serves 4

17 ounces/500 g baby spinach leaves
Maldon sea salt and ground white pepper
2 ounces/60 g pearl barley
1 quart/1 liter vegetable stock
2 baby artichokes
1 globe artichoke
Pinch Maldon sea salt
1 tablespoon white wine vinegar
7 tablespoons/100 g unsalted butter
4 cups/400 g rolled oats
2 zucchini, thinly grated
14 ounces/400 g spinach purée
3 ounces/80 g chives, finely snipped

7 ounces/200 g Parmesan cheese, grated
Juice of 2 lemons
5 tablespoons/80 g Normandy cream
 or crème fraîche
32 nasturtium leaves, to garnish
4 nasturtium flowers, to garnish
Extra virgin olive oil or chive oil
 (see page 183), to serve
Puffed barley (see page 211), to serve
Forest herb leaves (chervil, woodruff,
 mustard leaves, dill), to serve
3½ ounces/100 g roasted walnuts
 (see page 196)

MAKE THE SPINACH PURÉE

Bring a large pan of heavily salted water to a boil, then blanch the spinach leaves for about 30 seconds, remove, and refresh in ice-cold water. Squeeze excess water out of the spinach, reserving about 3 tablespoons. Transfer the spinach to a food processor or a blender and blend until smooth, gradually adding the reserved water until you have a thick, smooth paste.

COOK THE PEARL BARLEY & PREPARE THE ARTICHOKES

Cook the pearl barley in 1 cup/250 ml of the vegetable stock until just tender. Drain and set aside. Peel and prepare the artichokes (see page 157), placing them in a bowl of citric acid water. Slice the baby artichokes in half lengthwise and cut the globe artichoke heart into ½-inch/1-cm cubes. Bring a large pan of heavily salted water to a boil, add the vinegar, then blanch the artichokes for 5 to 10 minutes, until cooked through. Drain and set aside to cool until ready to serve.

MAKE THE RISOTTO

Melt the butter in a large saucepan. Add the oats and fry until browned and fragrant (but not too dark). Add the cooked barley and grated zucchini and sweat for 2 minutes, stirring. Add the remaining vegetable stock and cook for 10 minutes, stirring, until soft. Remove from the heat and stir in the spinach purée, chives, and Parmesan. Add the lemon juice, then season to taste. The risotto should be wet and bright green.

SERVE

Spoon some risotto onto each plate, then spoon cream or crème fraîche around it. Garnish with artichokes, then nasturtium leaves and flowers. Drizzle with olive oil or chive oil, scattering with puffed barley, forest herbs, and walnuts.

KING CRAB, WINTER RADISH, MUSHROOM, AND SEAWEED BROTH

King crab is my favorite of all the crabs. We have made many dishes with it at the Firehouse over the years, cooking it several ways. One of the best methods, in my opinion, is grilling it gently over a wood fire, brushing it constantly with our melted house-made butter. The smokiness and crisp exterior is quite amazing. If you have the time, and you have a wood-fired or charcoal grill, try this! Poaching it and pan-frying it—as we do here—works beautifully, too. You could swap the accompaniments below for seaweed-roasted new potatoes, lightly dressed greens, and the brown butter mayonnaise on page 128. King crab is expensive, so if you prefer, you can use other crabmeat, such as blue, stone, or Dungeness.

You need heat-proof plastic wrap for this recipe, which you can source online.

INGREDIENTS

Serves 4

FOR THE KOMBU:

½ ounce/15 g wild royal kombu leaves, broken into pieces
2½ cups/600 ml water
1 teaspoon shiro dashi
⅙ ounce/5 g fresh ginger, skin scraped off with a spoon and root sliced

FOR THE MUSHROOM STOCK

1⅔ cups/400 ml liquid from cooking the kombu
11 ounces/320 g button mushrooms, thinly sliced
4 teaspoons tawny port

9½ ounces/270 g meat from king crab claws, frozen or fresh, or other crabmeat (see headnote)
Unsalted butter
Maldon sea salt, to season
1⅓ ounces/40 g mixture of red radishes and daikon, very thinly sliced (we use a mandoline)
4 white button mushrooms, stems removed and mushrooms thinly sliced
4 green onions, thinly sliced into rounds on a mandoline
Extra virgin olive oil, for drizzling

CONTINUED

COOK THE KOMBU

Place all the ingredients in a large saucepan over medium heat, mix gently and bring to a boil, then immediately reduce the heat and simmer for 20 to 25 minutes, until the kombu is tender. Strain and reserve the kombu until you're ready to serve, reserving the strained liquid for the mushroom stock.

MAKE THE MUSHROOM STOCK

Pour ⅔ cup/150 ml of the liquid from cooking the kombu into a saucepan. Add the thinly sliced button mushrooms, bring to a boil, cover, and simmer for 30 minutes. Remove from the heat and leave to cool with the lid on, at room temperature. Once cooled, remove the mushrooms and strain the stock through a muslin-lined fine-mesh sieve or chinois. Add the port and mix thoroughly. (You can make this ahead of time, and store it in the fridge for up to 2 days.)

COOK THE CRAB

Bring a pan of water to a boil. Wrap the king crab claw meat in heat-proof plastic wrap, making sure it's watertight, then cook in the boiling water for 4 minutes. Remove the claw meat from the water, and plunge it straight into ice-cold water. Drain and remove the plastic wrap. When you're ready to serve, heat a frying pan until very hot, add a knob of butter and sear the meat, basting it with the butter. Remove the crab from the pan, brush with melted butter and season with a little salt.

SERVE

Warm 4 bowls. Divide the crabmeat into 4 portions, and put a portion in each bowl, adding a few drops of lemon juice if you wish. Add 4 thin slices of each radish variety, 4 thin slices of mushroom, 4 slices of green onion, and 3 pieces of kombu. Spoon a quarter of the mushroom stock over each serving. Drizzle with extra virgin olive oil to finish.

SEARED CUTTLEFISH WITH WHITE SPROUTING BROCCOLI AND BACON

You will have probably figured out by now that I am completely obsessed with seafood. Cuttlefish is one of my favorites, and the way we cook it at the Firehouse really brings out its flavor and gives it a wonderful texture.

The combination of land and sea in this dish is something I've been familiar with since my childhood growing up in Portugal. The smoky bacon broth works perfectly with the cuttlefish and broccoli, and in some strange way reminds me of some amazing incarnations of smoky, porky Southern-style greens in the U.S.

Ask your fishmonger to clean the cuttlefish for you, if you like, and save the trimmings and the tentacles (you could make a stock with the tentacles to use in a fish soup, or use the ink sacs and braised tentacles to make cuttlefish rice).

INGREDIENTS

Serves 4

2¼ pounds/1 kg Alsace bacon
  (or any smoky, fatty bacon),
  cut into ⅛-inch/2.5-mm dice
2 tablespoons unsalted butter
1 sheet royal kombu
3¼ pounds/1.5 kg cuttlefish, cleaned
  (ask your fishmonger to do this
  for you, if you prefer), or fresh,
  large squid
1⅓ pounds/600 g white sprouting
  broccoli, if you can find it, or purple
  sprouting broccoli, stalks trimmed
  and leaves retained

2 cups/500 ml grapeseed oil,
  plus extra for frying the cuttlefish
⅙ ounce/5 g kuzu (optional)
White soy sauce, to season
Citron vinegar, to season
Extra virgin olive oil, for drizzling
Maldon sea salt and freshly ground
  black pepper
2 teaspoons English mustard powder,
  to season

CONTINUED

MAKE THE BACON BROTH

Preheat the oven to its lowest setting and line a baking sheet with parchment paper. Place the diced bacon in a frying pan over medium heat, add just enough water to cover, and cook, stirring and occasionally skimming off any foam that forms on the surface. When all the water has evaporated (this takes 10 to 15 minutes), add the butter and keep stirring as the butter melts and foams. When the bacon is dark golden brown, remove from the heat, pass through a sieve to strain off the fat (you can reserve the fat to use in other recipes if you wish) and drain the bacon bits on paper towels to remove excess butter and fat. Place the bacon bits on the lined tray and bake for 30 minutes, until dehydrated and crispy. Transfer the bacon bits to a pan on the stove top, cover with about 1 quart/1 liter of water, add the kombu, and simmer over low heat for 2½ hours. Pass through a fine-mesh sieve into a heatproof bowl and leave to cool.

PREPARE THE CUTTLEFISH

Remove the skin, ink sacs, and tentacles from the cuttlefish or squid—you should be left with 1¾ to 2¼ pounds/800 to 1000 g of flesh.

Cut the cuttlefish into 4 equal-sized "steaks" (7 to 9 ounces/200 to 250 g each). Score the undersides in a criss-cross pattern and pat dry thoroughly with paper towels.

Prepare the broccoli two ways (blanched and fried).

Blanch half of the trimmed broccoli and the broccoli leaves in generously salted boiling water for 3 minutes (it needs to be crunchy, not soft). Drain and set aside at room temperature.

Heat the grapeseed oil in a deep saucepan over high heat. For the fried broccoli, trim the stalks further so you're left with just the florets and a small stump of stalk, then deep-fry for about 45 seconds. Remove with a slotted spoon, and transfer to paper towels. Season well with salt and pepper and keep warm.

COOK THE CUTTLEFISH

Heat a frying pan until very hot, then add a generous drizzle of grapeseed oil and sear the cuttlefish, sprinkled with salt, one "steak" at a time, covering the cuttlefish with a heavy weight while it cooks (to prevent it curling), for about 2 minutes on each side, then remove from the pan and set aside to rest before you serve. If you like, you can rub the ink from the ink sacs all over the cuttlefish before serving.

SERVE

Warm 4 bowls. Reheat the bacon broth, adding the kuzu, if using, and seasoning it with white soy and citron vinegar to taste. Carve the rested cuttlefish into thin slices and place some in the bottom of each bowl. Season the blanched broccoli with extra virgin olive oil, salt, and pepper, then place on top of the cuttlefish. Top with the fried broccoli, then spoon 7 tablespoons/100 ml of reheated bacon broth into the bowls and sprinkle with the mustard powder. Serve immediately.

ROASTED JERUSALEM ARTICHOKES WITH HAZELNUT DRESSING

Jerusalem artichokes (also known as sunchokes) are an ingredient that I remember my father raving about when I was young, back in Portugal. Sometimes, when they were in season, he'd make a very special soup with them, slicing them thinly and cooking them in a rich meat stock with vegetables and herbs, toasted bread, and poached eggs. We only ate it once or twice a year but it was quite a ceremony. Soon after moving back to Europe from the U.S., my love affair with this treasure of nature returned and I experimented with it on my restaurant menus, trying different cooking techniques and serving them savory or sweet. At the Firehouse, we cook them with plenty of foaming butter then smoke them on the grill. The result is amazing.

NUNO'S TIP
This dish requires black truffle and Jerusalem artichokes, so is best made at the end of winter when they are both in season and at their best.

INGREDIENTS

Serves 6

10 ounces/300 g Stracciatella, ricotta, or another clean-flavored soft cheese
2¼ cups/500 g unsalted butter
12 large, smooth Jerusalem artichokes (2 per person), washed thoroughly and dried

FOR THE HAZELNUT DRESSING:

5½ ounces/160 g skinless hazelnuts
6 tablespoons/90 ml Chardonnay vinegar (we use the Forum brand)

2 ounces/65 g shallots, thinly diced
⅔ cup/160 ml hazelnut oil

FOR THE JERUSALEM ARTICHOKE JUS:

14 ounces/400 g Jerusalem artichokes
⅙ ounce/5 g black truffle paste

⅕ ounce/6 g fresh black truffle, for grating

TAKE THE CHEESE OUT OF THE FRIDGE

You need to serve it at room temperature.

ROAST THE ARTICHOKES

You will need a 6-inch/15-cm-deep saucepan or pot with a surface area large enough to fit the artichokes in one layer with a little bit of room between them.

Add a few tablespoons of the butter to the pan over medium heat and cook it for about 5 minutes, whisking continuously, until brown, nutty, and fragrant, making sure it doesn't burn. Once it is brown and the bubbles start to disappear, add the artichokes and coat them in the butter. Reduce the heat a little, then add the remaining butter a little at a time, until it is all melted and foaming in the pan. The key is to keep the butter foaming the whole time. Keep turning the artichokes every few minutes, cooking them for about 30 minutes, or until they start to almost collapse. Test them with a metal skewer: they should be cooked through and hot in the center. Transfer the artichokes to a baking sheet, spoon over the roasting juices, and leave them to cool slightly while you prepare the dressing and garnishes.

CONTINUED

MAKE THE HAZELNUT DRESSING

Preheat the oven to 325°F/160°C. Spread the hazelnuts out on a baking sheet and bake for about 20 minutes, shaking the tray after 10 minutes then returning it to the oven, until the nuts are golden and fragrant. Remove from the oven and leave to cool, then roughly crush the nuts in a mortar and pestle. Bring the vinegar to a boil in a small saucepan and add the shallots. Remove from the heat, allow to cool, then whisk in the oil and add the roasted hazelnuts just before you're ready to serve. Leave the oven on.

MAKE THE JERUSALEM ARTICHOKE JUS

Wash the artichokes and juice them using a juicer. Put the artichoke juice in a pan over medium heat and boil for 3 to 4 minutes until reduced by a third. Pour the juice through a fine-mesh sieve into a bowl, clean the pan, and put the juice back in. Repeat the process, reducing the jus by another third over medium heat. Strain and return the jus to the cleaned-out pan and whisk in the black truffle paste. You should have ⅔ to ¾ cup/150 to 200 ml of jus. Keep warm.

SERVE

Warm 6 bowls. Warm the artichokes through in the oven, cut them in half lengthwise, then place in the serving bowls, spooning over the artichoke jus. Cover the artichokes with the soft cheese and a few tablespoons of the hazelnut dressing. Grate as much black truffle as you like over the top and serve immediately while the dish is warm and aromatic.

ALVIS NEMIRO

Sommelier

I grew up in Riga, the capital of Latvia, but my summers were always spent in the countryside, foraging, fruit-picking, learning about the tastes and smells of nature.

On my sixteenth birthday, my grandfather sat me down and said, "It's time for you to try a fine wine." It was a Burgundy. I didn't really get it, but I just loved the way he described it to me, and the story of how and where he got the bottle.

My family was made up of scientists and engineers, but I decided to study music and fashion. I was playing in a psychedelic garage rock-funk band. To pay the bills, I worked in an Italian restaurant. The chef really opened my mind to both food and wine.

FIREHOUSE DISCOVERIES
Three California wineries: Araujo, which was recently acquired by Château Latour; Diamond Creek; and Dumol.

PAIRINGS
Our pine-roasted monkfish with a 2006 Blanc de Negres de Capçanes. This is a Spanish white wine made from red garnacha grapes and has enormous complexity and depth, and enough power to complement smoky, meaty monkfish. Also, cornbread with 2012 Dumol Chloé Chardonnay. Butter on butter!

BABY ARTICHOKES, FRESH RICOTTA, HERBED RYE, AND LARDO

I love artichokes but they tend not to be the easiest ingredient to build a dish around. When I first created this dish, while trialing recipes for the Firehouse, we made the ricotta ourselves; it was really special but very labor-intensive for a low yield. So we shelved it until restaurant operations allowed us to make fresh ricotta daily. Just as we were happy with production, our friends at Neal's Yard Dairy introduced us to a product they were developing, a lovely fresh ricotta using Westcombe Cheddar curds and whey. This was a great alternative that would save manpower and production space, but I still have dreams about our just-made warm, fresh, and sweet ricotta.

Unless you are serving an army, try to make ricotta at home—you may find a new calling and decide to make cheese for a living!

This recipe makes more lemon purée than you need, but it needn't go to waste—you can add honey to it and serve it with cake or toasted brioche, or turn it into lemon curd.

INGREDIENTS

Serves 4

FOR THE CARAWAY BUTTER:

6 tablespoons/40 g caraway seeds
¾ cup/170 g unsalted butter

FOR THE SPINACH & CHIVE PURÉE:

1½ pounds/700 g cooked and
 drained spinach
½ ounce/15 g chives
6 tablespoons/85 g caraway butter

FOR THE LEMON PURÉE:

2 unwaxed lemons
2½ tablespoons honey
1½ tablespoons extra virgin olive oil
Salt and ground white pepper

1 tablespoon citric acid, dissolved in
 1 quart/1 liter cold water
4 baby artichokes
1 cup/250 ml green olive juice (from
 1 quart/1 liter brined green olives)
7 ounces/200 g rye bread, thinly sliced
8 tablespoons/125 g fresh ricotta
3½ ounces/100 g lardo, shaved very
 thinly, until almost translucent
Handful chickweed or chervil
Extra virgin olive oil
Maldon sea salt and black pepper,
 to season

MAKE THE CARAWAY BUTTER

Toast the caraway seeds in a dry frying pan until fragrant, then add the butter. Increase the heat until the butter has melted and is bubbling, then transfer the caraway butter to a blender and blend for 1 minute to break up the seeds. Transfer to a bowl and leave to infuse for 2 hours, then strain through a fine-mesh sieve into a bowl to remove the seeds. Cover and set aside somewhere warm.

CONTINUED

MAKE THE SPINACH & CHIVE PURÉE

Blend the cooked spinach and chives in a food processor or blender until they form a purée. Gently heat the caraway butter until it is warm again, then slowly pour it into the purée, with the motor still running, to form an emulsion. Strain through a fine-mesh sieve into a bowl and season to taste. Cover and set aside at room temperature.

MAKE THE LEMON PURÉE

Place the lemons in a saucepan, cover with cold water, and bring to a boil, then remove them and rinse them under cold running water until they are cold. Put them back in the pan. Boil and cool them 3 times, each time starting with fresh cold water. On the third and final boil, keep them in the boiling water for about 20 minutes, until the lemons are soft. Drain, leave to cool, then cut the lemons in half, scoop out the pulp with a spoon and put it in a fine-mesh sieve over a bowl. Push the pulp through the sieve and discard the seeds. Remove the white pith from the skin and discard, then chop the skin coarsely and add it to the lemon juice and pulp.

Place the honey, lemon pulp, and skin in a pan and boil for 1 minute. Transfer to a blender or the bowl of a food processor and blend until smooth, then slowly pour in the oil until the purée is emulsified. Season with salt and pepper to taste, cover, and chill until ready to use.

PREPARE THE ARTICHOKE

Divide the citric acid water between three separate containers. Strip away the tough outer leaves of one of the artichokes with a small paring knife and cut off the top to expose the white heart (make sure you leave about 1¼ inches/3 cm between the leaf and the stalk, and that you don't break the stem). Place the outer leaves in the first container. Peel away the inner leaves, placing them in a second container, until you reach the artichoke heart, making sure you leave a rim of leaves around the edge, and peel the stem. Place the artichoke heart and stem in the third container. Carve the stem and remove the hairy fibers (choke) from the top of the heart and return to the third container. Repeat with the remaining artichokes.

COOK THE ARTICHOKE

Put the trimmed artichoke hearts in a small saucepan and cover them with the green olive juice. Cover with a cartouche (a circle of parchment paper or greaseproof paper cut to the same size as the pan) so that none of the artichokes are exposed to the air.

Poach them gently for 25 minutes over low to medium heat, until tender but still retaining bite. Remove the pan from the heat, leaving them in the liquid.

TOAST & SOAK THE BREAD

Lightly toast 2 slices of rye bread per person then place half of it—retaining the rest to garnish—in a shallow container. Pour the spinach and chive purée over the hot bread and leave it to soak at room temperature for about 2 hours, or until the liquid is absorbed and it all becomes a mushy, crumbly mix. Season with salt then set aside at room temperature.

SERVE

Chill 4 serving plates. Spoon 2 tablespoons of fresh ricotta onto each cold plate, top with a quartered artichoke, then spoon over some of the spinach-rye mixture and a couple of dots of the lemon purée.

Garnish with shavings of fresh lardo, thin shavings of the reserved toasted rye bread, and a sprinkling of chickweed of chervil. Drizzle with a little extra virgin olive oil and season with a couple of twists of black pepper.

CAJUN QUAIL

Although I never lived in the American South (except for Miami, which is worlds apart from other southern states), I did—during my years in North America—enjoy the Cajun flavors of Louisiana and the honest cooking from the Carolinas, Mississippi, and Alabama. This dish closely resembles what could be referred to as "real" Southern American cooking. Cajun spices always work well with poultry, and this quail is perfect for serving at a barbecue with cocktails or an ice-cold beer on a balmy summer evening.

INGREDIENTS

Serves 4

FOR THE ALMOND YOGURT:

¾ cup/200 g thick Greek yogurt
3½ tablespoons almond milk
1 teaspoon almond oil
Maldon sea salt, to season

FOR THE CAJUN SPICE MARINADE:

6 tablespoons/40 g smoked paprika, plus extra to garnish
4 teaspoons onion powder
5 teaspoons dried oregano (Mexican, if you can find it)
2 teaspoons cayenne pepper
1 teaspoon Maldon sea salt
4 teaspoons freshly ground black pepper

1¼ cups/300 ml grapeseed oil, plus 2 tablespoons for searing the quail
4 quail

FOR THE LEMON DRESSING:

1 tablespoon freshly squeezed lemon juice
4½ teaspoons light soy sauce
2 tablespoons extra virgin olive oil
Maldon sea salt and freshly ground black pepper, to taste

1¾ pounds/800 g salad leaves
¾ cup/200 ml lemon dressing
7 ounces/200 g toasted almonds, halved or cut into slivers
3½ ounces/100 g preserved lemon rind, thinly sliced

Paprika, to serve

CONTINUED

MAKE THE ALMOND YOGURT	Whisk all of the ingredients together until the oil is emulsified. Adjust with salt to taste. Cover and chill until ready to serve.

MARINATE THE QUAIL	Mix all of the Cajun spice marinade ingredients with ¾ cup/200 ml of the grapeseed oil. Place the quail in a bowl and add half the marinade and the remaining grapeseed oil. Cover, transfer to the fridge, and leave to marinate for 2 to 4 hours. Retain the remaining marinade for basting.

COOK THE QUAIL	Preheat the oven to 350°F/180°C. Heat the 2 tablespoons of grapeseed oil in a frying pan over high heat until hot, then sear the marinated quail for 1 minute on each side. Place the quail breast side down in a roasting pan and transfer to the oven to roast for 8 to 10 minutes until a probe thermometer inserted into the breast meat reads 145°F/63°C. Remove from the oven, leave to rest for 5 minutes, then cut each quail into two pieces down the middle, so each half has a leg and a thigh and some breast. Baste the quail with the remaining marinade, retaining 3 or 4 tablespoons to serve.

SERVE	Chill 4 plates. Make the lemon dressing by mixing the ingredients together and seasoning with salt and pepper. Toss the salad leaves with ¾ cup/200 ml of the lemon dressing, then sprinkle with toasted almonds and preserved lemon rind.

Onto each cold plate, place 2 tablespoons of the almond yogurt, 2 quail halves, and a drizzle of the reserved marinade. Add a sprinkling of paprika to the yogurt and serve with the tossed leaves. |

SMOKED EEL WITH POTATO SALAD

Ever since I moved to London and started eating at St. John Bread and Wine, I have fallen in love with British-style smoked eel. Although I've eaten eel in Japanese restaurants for years, eel in the UK is totally different, and I actually prefer it. The fattiness and smokiness works wonderfully with the lactic sourness of crème fraîche. It is now one of my favorite dishes and when I see it on a menu, I always order it.

Remember never to discard the trimmings, skin, and bones of the eel (if you're able to buy it whole)—they are amazing for flavoring broths and sauces.

INGREDIENTS

Serves 4

FOR THE PICKLED ONIONS:

1¼ cups/300 ml water
¾ cup/200 ml white wine vinegar
½ cup/100 g superfine sugar
20 pearl onions, peeled and washed

8 ounces/240 g whole smoked eel,
  or smoked eel fillets
1 shallot, sliced
2 sprigs thyme

FOR THE POTATO SALAD:

12 La Ratte or other fingerling
  potatoes, peeled and cut into
  ½-inch/1-cm-thick slices
1 quart/1 liter fresh fish stock
  (if you have no eel bones/trimmings
  to make eel stock)
2 tablespoons finely chopped shallot
1 tablespoon finely snipped chives
1 tablespoon finely chopped flat-leaf
  parsley leaves
Maldon sea salt and freshly ground
  black pepper, to taste
3 tablespoons extra virgin olive oil,
  plus extra to serve

4 tablespoons crème fraîche, to serve
Wood sorrel or regular sorrel,
  to garnish
Nasturtium leaves, to garnish

PICKLE THE ONIONS

Heat the water, vinegar, and sugar in a saucepan until the sugar has dissolved. Add the onions and cook over low heat (do not boil) for 10 minutes. Remove the pan from the heat and set aside, allowing the onions to cool in the pickling liquid. Transfer the onions and liquid to an airtight container, seal, and store in the fridge until ready to serve (the onions keep well in the fridge for up to 2 weeks).

PREPARE THE EEL

Preheat the oven to 300°F/150°C. If you have a whole eel, remove the fillets from the eel in one length: place the eel on a chopping board, pierce through the skin with a sharp knife at the head end, next to the backbone, and cut along the backbone from head to tail. Cut all the way to the end of the belly near the tail, then gently pull the bone away with your hands. Place the fillets on a baking sheet. Warm them on the skin

CONTINUED

side with a blowtorch (or briefly in the oven) so that the layer of fat between the skin and the flesh softens, then peel away the skin from the tail end to the head end. It should come off very easily. Save the skin for making the broth and cut the fillets into 1-inch/2.5-cm-thick slices.

Place the eel bones in a roasting pan and bake in the oven for 40 minutes. Remove from the oven and transfer the bones to a large saucepan, breaking them up a bit so that they fit in. Pour in twice the amount of water as the weight of eel bones, bring to a simmer, add the shallot and thyme, and cook, uncovered, for 1 hour, skimming off any froth that forms on the surface. Add the skins and cook for a further 30 minutes. Remove from the heat and pour the eel stock through a fine-mesh sieve into another pan.

PREPARE THE POTATOES

Cook the potatoes in the eel stock (or fresh fish stock) at just below simmering point (don't boil) for about 25 minutes, or until they are just tender but still have a little bit of bite. Remove from the heat and allow to cool in the stock.

Drain the potatoes (retaining a few tablespoons of the stock) and place them in a bowl. Add the shallot, chives, parsley, and salt and pepper to taste, then add the olive oil and a little of the reserved eel stock to loosen the salad again. Set aside at room temperature until ready to serve.

SERVE

Warm 4 bowls. Add a few tablespoons of olive oil and a few tablespoons of eel or fish stock to the potato salad again. Arrange the potatoes in the bowls, warm the pieces of eel in the oven and add to the bowls. Add 1 tablespoon of crème fraîche to each bowl, scatter with 6 to 8 pieces of pickled onion and dress with sorrel and nasturtium leaves. Serve immediately.

GRILLED OCTOPUS, EGGPLANT, DAIKON, AND MUSHROOMS

Octopus is truly a Portuguese ingredient. I have been eating it since my early childhood in Portugal, and must have tried it prepared in a thousand ways. Some years ago, however, in my travels through Asia, I remember tasting an octopus dish that inspired me to look at the cephalopod in a completely different way, considering different flavor partners to the typical Portuguese or Galician ones. Some of the classic Japanese cooking traditions have their origins in Portugal, and this dish illustrates that close connection between the Japanese and the Portuguese palate.

INGREDIENTS

Serves 8 (1 tentacle per person)

FOR THE TOASTED SUNFLOWER SEEDS:

1 ounce/30 g sunflower seeds
1 teaspoon fish sauce
½ teaspoon superfine sugar

FOR THE OCTOPUS BASTING OIL:

6 tablespoons/90 ml extra virgin olive oil
⅕ ounce/6 g garlic cloves
1/14 ounce/2 g red chile, seeded and chopped
1/10 ounce/3 g Maldon sea salt
⅙ ounce/5 g cilantro stalks, thinly chopped
Grated zest of 1 unwaxed lemon

FOR THE AGA DASHI:

3 cups/750 ml water
1 tablespoon hon dashi
2 tablespoons light soy sauce
¼ cup/60 ml mirin
3 tablespoons shiro dashi
2 teaspoons superfine sugar
⅙ ounce/5 g piece dried royal kombu

FOR THE BRAISED KOMBU:

7 ounces/200 g fresh royal kombu
5 teaspoons shiro dashi
4 cups/950 ml water
2 tablespoons superfine sugar
⅓ ounce/10 g fresh ginger, peeled and grated
4 teaspoons low-salt soy sauce
3 to 4 teaspoons white rice vinegar

14 ounces/400 g daikon, cubed
⅙ ounce/5 g bonito flakes

FOR THE EGGPLANT PURÉE

2 cups/500 ml grapeseed oil, for deep-frying
1 eggplant
⅓ cup/60 g rice flour

FOR THE OCTOPUS MARINATING OIL:

1⅔ cups/400 ml extra virgin olive oil
1 teaspoon sweet smoked paprika
1 teaspoon Maldon sea salt

FOR THE OCTOPUS:

1 large octopus (4⅓ to 5½ pounds/2 to 2.5 kg), or 2 smaller octopus, frozen (or freeze after purchase if bought fresh)
7 tablespoons/100 ml grapeseed oil
3 onions, sliced
3 cloves garlic, thinly sliced
5 bay leaves
4 teaspoons sweet smoked paprika
1⅔ cups/375 ml white wine

FOR THE MUSHROOMS:

Unsalted butter
1⅓ ounces/40 g hon shimeji mushooms, stems removed
¾ ounce/20 g shiitake mushrooms, quartered
1 tablespoon mirin
Low-salt soy sauce, to taste

CONTINUED

TOAST THE SUNFLOWER SEEDS	Preheat the oven to 325°F/160°C and line a baking sheet with parchment paper. Mix all the ingredients in a bowl. Spread the mixture out on the lined baking sheet and bake for 8 to 12 minutes. Remove after the first 2 minutes and—wearing heatproof gloves—rub the seeds to separate them and spread them evenly over the tray. Continue to bake for the remaining time, then remove from the oven and set aside.
MAKE THE OCTOPUS BASTING OIL & AGA DASHI	Heat 3½ tablespoons of the oil in a saucepan, add the garlic, chile, and salt and fry for 6 minutes, until softened, then add the remaining oil and gently warm it until it reaches 175°F/80°C. Add the remaining basting oil ingredients, stir, remove from the heat, and leave to infuse. Place all the ingredients for the aga dashi in a saucepan, bring to a boil, remove from the heat, and leave to infuse at room temperature for 4 hours.
MAKE THE BRAISED KOMBU	Place all the ingredients except the bonito flakes in a large saucepan. Bring to a boil, reduce the heat, and simmer gently for 45 minutes, or until the kombu and daikon are tender. Remove from the heat, add the bonito flakes, and chill until ready to serve.
MAKE THE EGGPLANT PURÉE	Heat the oil in a deep saucepan until it reaches 355°F/180°C. Peel the eggplant, cut it into small cubes, and toss in the rice flour to coat. Deep-fry for 3 to 4 minutes until golden brown. Place the fried eggplant cubes in a container with enough aga dashi to cover it and leave for 2 hours, then purée in a food processor, adding more aga dashi if necessary, until you have a thick, spoonable purée. Chill until ready to serve.
MAKE THE OCTOPUS MARINATING OIL & COOK THE OCTOPUS	Combine the ingredients in a container big enough to contain the octopus. Set aside. Wash the octopus thoroughly in cold water and remove its beak. Heat the oil in a large, deep stainless steel saucepan, add the onions, garlic, bay, and paprika and cook until they take on some color and brown slightly. Add the octopus and stir, covering the octopus in the aromatics, then add the wine and bring to a boil. Reduce the heat to a gentle simmer, cover, and cook for 40 to 60 minutes, until the octopus is tender. Remove it from the pan, carefully cut the tentacles away from the body, and place in the container of marinating oil. Pass the cooking liquor through a fine-mesh sieve into a clean bowl, cover, and chill.
COOK THE MUSHROOMS	Heat the butter in a frying pan. Add the mushrooms and cook gently for 3 to 4 minutes, until cooked through. Add the mirin, then add soy sauce to taste. Increase the heat until the mushrooms are lightly colored, remove from the pan, and keep warm.
GRILL THE OCTOPUS	Before serving, briefly sear the octopus tentacles in a nonstick frying pan over high heat, in a little of the oil they were marinated in, turning them and basting them to give them a nice smoky crust.
SERVE	Warm the plates. Spoon 2 tablespoons of eggplant purée onto each plate. Top with octopus and scatter with mushrooms, sunflower seeds, daikon, and kombu. Spoon a little basting oil over the octopus and serve immediately.

MAINS

IN THE KITCHEN

Nuno Mendes

I COME FROM LISBON, and the sea is in the blood of the Portuguese. For hundreds of years my ancestors explored the oceans, discovering half the world for Europe. My dream as a boy was to be a deep sea explorer like my hero, Jacques Cousteau.

So I moved to Miami in the early nineties to study marine biology. I soon discovered this was not for me. But Miami Beach, where I lived, was an interesting scene. There were lots of good Asian and European restaurants, along with huge Cuban and Nicaraguan communities. My step-mom was Nicaraguan, so I already knew a bit about Nicaraguan food. I loved being part of this multiethnic community, where food and cooking expressed so much of one's identity. My girlfriend at the time gave me a cookbook. It was published by the California Culinary Academy. I soon learned that it was California that was the real melting pot of nationalities and cuisines. That was where everything seemed to be happening, so I enrolled in the Culinary Academy.

Before I went to California, I had to honor a promise to my father: that I would return to Portugal and work on the dairy farm that had been in our family for generations. Shifting from Miami to a sleepy farm in Alentejo was not what my twenty-two-year-old self really wanted to do. But it taught me so much about the food chain—about animals and their products, what sustainable agriculture is, and about Iberico pork in particular; what we serve at the Firehouse comes from the

same acorn-eating pigs that I first saw in Alentejo. When I arrived in California nine months later, I knew more about food than most of my classmates. I just didn't know that much about cooking. But I loved school from day one. The intoxicating smells, the excitement

Thirty-five covers, a fridge, no freezers, everything came in fresh, the menu changed every week.

of the busy kitchen, learning about table service, about wine, about running a restaurant. I had found my passion. After graduating, I went to work in a small restaurant on Thirteenth and Mission called Woodward's Garden, run by two wonderful ladies. It was a rough area in 1995 but it was a great apprenticeship. Thirty-five covers, a fridge, no freezers, everything came in fresh, the menu changed every week: five, five, five—five starters, five mains, five desserts. The next week we would start over with a different menu depending on what was fresh.

Almost everything was locally sourced. I learned so much because it was such a small operation. We would take perfect peaches and a little goats' cheese and sit them on a bed of beautiful greens, lightly tossed with a little olive oil and lemon juice, and finished with a really good-quality prosciutto and a little pecan crumbled over the top for crunch. Simple, simple, simple. It was such a great education for someone straight out of cooking school.

I had a friend who was working at Postrio, Wolfgang Puck's new restaurant in San Francisco. He got me a trial and I was blown away. I felt like I was back in school. It was where I really developed as a chef. I spent almost three years there.

Postrio was a large restaurant and a very complex operation. There were whole two-hundred-plus-pound tuna coming through the door, whole lambs we would butcher ourselves. We made our own bagels, chocolate cookies, terrines, pasta, gnocchi—everything. The chefs were incredibly talented. Everyone seemed to come from a different place in the world and they all had their own culinary history, which they were excited to share. That's something that I've always believed in and have carried with me into the Firehouse: the conversation among chefs and the front of house, everyone talking to each other. I don't want my kitchen to be a dictatorship. We always discuss and taste things collectively, thinking about how we can improve, which is the way Wolfgang works.

Around 1999 I spent a week in New York. The whole scene really excited me, so not long after I packed my bags and moved east. A couple of chef friends from Postrio were already working for Rocco DiSpirito at Union Pacific and got me in there. Rocco had the best product I'd ever seen. I'd never encountered white truffles as large as in that kitchen. And there were four or five different types of caviar in the fridge. And real wasabi root flown in from Japan, which I'd never encountered before. He was the man of the moment, thirty-two years old and super passionate. It was rock and roll. The energy in that kitchen was very special, but also brutal. Everybody was trying to be really tough like Rocco and if you didn't measure up, you dropped out. Knives were thrown, people yelled, there were even fistfights. It was uncompromising: the dish went out perfect, or not at all. And if

It was rock and roll. The energy in that kitchen was very special.

someone was not on his game the whole place would turn on him. There were a lot of young kids who all wanted to prove themselves. But gradually this constant battle became a toxic atmosphere for me. I felt we could have been doing so much more if the atmosphere had been more positive, helping each other rather than judging. I loved the restaurant but hated the environment. I told Rocco, "I think your food is amazing but this is not a nice place to work and I can't get excited about being here anymore." He asked me to stay but it was too late for me. Rocco was truly inspiring in his energy and passion, the quality of the ingredients, the lack of any compromise. But ultimately the lesson I left with was how I didn't want a kitchen to run. I believe you can achieve perfection in a civilized environment. This is the key for me to running a restaurant. You and your staff need to wake

If your team can see how your guests are reacting to the food it makes them feel good.

up in the morning excited about coming to work. That's why I like open kitchens. If your team can see how the guests are reacting to the food it makes them feel good and they want to do their best for the customers. It's a virtuous circle. The guest can feel if a place is happy and successful.

When I left Rocco, my girlfriend at the time wanted to go to New Mexico and study jewelery design. I managed to get into Mark Miller's restaurant, the Coyote Café, in Santa Fe. Mark was one of the first to introduce Southwestern cuisine as a concept and style of cooking. Working there gave me another piece of my culinary puzzle. Some of the best ingredients from all over Latin America arrived in our kitchen daily. Mark knows more about food than anyone I've ever met. He would travel to Peru, Japan, Vietnam, and bring back these extraordinary ingredients. His knowledge of food and culture was beyond anything I had ever encountered. We had fifty or sixty different types of chiles and we would make lots of different versions of moles every day. We made tamales, we made tacos, we made enchiladas, we would grind all our own meats. We dry-aged our beef and hung our own pork. The technique for the sauces was very interesting: lots of refrying—something completely different from the French style of cooking I had found in New York or California. Working with Mark was a very happy accident. I had no plan to go to New Mexico, but when I wound up there I fell in love with the place.

I had the opportunity to spend a month at the legendary El Bulli in Spain, which was regarded as the best restaurant in the world. What can I say about Ferran? He gave me the confidence to follow my dreams. To create a restaurant based on an experience. A place where it's not just a service, it's an artistic expression, creating an emotional journey. I think people overemphasize the technical and "molecular" aspects of what Ferran was cooking. Actually he was creating a total experience that began before you even arrived at the restaurant. Travelling to that beautiful coast, the myth of the restaurant in your mind, breathing the smell of the sea as you approached, the thrill of trying something completely new.

Back in New York, I spent a year working for Jean-Georges Vongerichten in his flagship restaurant. He was a gentleman, and he understood how to treat his staff. His food was super-tasty, thoughtful, clever. He was one of the first modern chefs to understand how you can put three ingredients on a plate, and if they're great ingredients, the dish will be great. It was different from the California method; it wasn't just farm to table. With Jean-Georges there is always a chef's touch, which means a layering of flavors. It was a little like an old-school French kitchen—reliable, perfected, efficient—but with a contemporary New York flair. I loved how he brought Asian ingredients into his cooking. He was the first guy to bring Thai and Vietnamese flavors into modern French cooking. He captured the fragrance and lightness of eating in Asia, but mingled it with French technique. Soy sauce, loads of fresh herbs, natural juices, almost no butter—at the time, these were all very progressive ideas. It led me to want to discover more

What can I say about Ferran? He gave me the confidence to follow my dreams. To create a restaurant based on an experience.

about these flavors myself, so I wound up traveling through Asia for five months, learning at every turn. When I got back to New York, George Bush won the re-election and I felt my time in the States had come to an end. I said "I'm out of here," and that was it. The next week, I moved to London.

ROASTED CELERIAC, SPROUTING BROCCOLI, PEARL ONIONS, AND WALNUTS

We go to great lengths at the Firehouse to make sure our vegetarian guests do not feel like second-class citizens. For many years I have dined out with vegetarian friends and found that their options were far more limited than mine; it often seems like vegetarian options are an afterthought. We offer what we believe are creative and super-tasty dishes that will not only satisfy an empty tummy, but will also satisfy the curious foodie soul.

This complex dish has lots of different textures. The celeriac is first salt-baked to retain its moisture and cook it evenly, then pan-roasted and basted in foaming butter until golden brown and delicious. This treatment can be applied to other root vegetables, such as parsnips, beets, and rutabagas, too. Prepare all the garnishes—the leaves, onion, broccoli, and celeriac ribbons—beforehand. They'll happily sit at room temperature for a few hours while you focus your full attention on the celeriac.

INGREDIENTS

Serves 4

FOR THE SALT-BAKED CELERIAC:

2 small celeriac, or 1 large
  (3¼-pound/1.5-kg) celeriac,
  scrubbed clean
8 cups/1.1 kg all-purpose flour
3 cups/900 g fine table salt
2½ cups/600 ml water
5 tablespoons/70 ml vegetable oil

FOR THE HAZELNUT & CHERVIL DRESSING:

4 teaspoons Dijon mustard
2 free-range egg yolks
1 tablespoon white wine vinegar
½ cup/125 ml grapeseed oil
7 tablespoons/100 ml hazelnut oil
3½ ounces/100 g chervil leaves,
  washed and drained
Maldon sea salt and freshly ground
  black pepper

FOR THE CELERIAC RIBBONS & MILK:

1 raw celeriac, peeled
3½ tablespoons unsalted butter
⅓ ounce/9 g salt
1¼ cups/300 ml whole milk
7 tablespoons/100 ml heavy cream
7 tablespoons/100 ml celery juice
  (made with a juicer)

FOR THE ROASTED ONIONS:

6 red onions
Red wine vinegar, for dressing
Maldon sea salt and freshly ground
  black pepper

FOR THE PINE OR ROSEMARY OIL:

7 tablespoons/100 ml grapeseed oil
2 ounces/60 g pine needles or fresh
  rosemary leaves
4 ounces/125 g spinach leaves

TO FINISH:

2 tablespoons unsalted butter
8 roasted walnuts
12 tips purple sprouting broccoli,
  blanched
12 sprigs chervil
¼ cup/60 g crème fraîche

CONTINUED

BAKE THE CELERIAC IN THE SALT DOUGH

Preheat the oven to 350°F/180°C and pat the celeriac dry with paper towels.

Combine the flour and salt in a large bowl. Gradually pour in the water, incorporating it into the flour, then add the oil. Knead to form a smooth dough (if it is dry and cracking, add a little more water; if it's wet and sticky, add a little more flour). Allow to rest for 20 minutes.

Roll the dough out into a ½-inch/1-cm-thick sheet. Place the celeriac on the dough and gently work the dough around the celeriac, forming an even layer that completely encases it (or wrap 2 smaller celeriac separately in the dough). Place on a baking sheet and cook in the oven for about 1½ hours. We test its doneness with a probe thermometer—its internal temperature needs to reach 165°F/75°C.

Remove from the oven and allow to cool for 20 to 30 minutes.

Crack open the salt dough shell, being careful not to damage the celeriac inside. Cut each celeriac into 6 wedges (or one large one into 12 wedges) and remove the skin. Set aside at room temperature.

MAKE THE HAZELNUT & CHERVIL DRESSING

Combine the mustard, egg yolks, and vinegar in a bowl, then gradually drizzle in both the oils, whisking continuously, until emulsified. Transfer to a blender or the bowl of a food processor, add the chervil, and blend for 5 minutes, until bright green and smooth. Pass through a fine-mesh sieve into a bowl and season with salt and pepper.

MAKE THE CELERIAC RIBBONS & MILK

Using a mandoline, thinly slice the raw celeriac into strips, then cut them down to make about sixteen 1 by 4-inch/2.5 by 10-cm ribbons. Set the ribbons aside and keep the trimmings.

Melt the butter in a saucepan, then add 3½ ounces/100 g of the celeriac trimmings with the salt. Cover the pan with heatproof plastic wrap and cook over very low heat for 6 to 7 minutes so the celeriac releases its juices. Remove the plastic wrap, add the milk and cream to the celeriac and return to the heat until the mixture reaches 160°F/70°C on a probe thermometer. Remove from the heat, cover the pan with plastic wrap again, and leave to infuse for 15 minutes, then pass through a fine-mesh sieve into a heatproof bowl. Leave to cool, then transfer to the fridge. When the mixture is cold, add the celery juice.

Bring a pan of lightly salted water (2 teaspoons salt to 1 quart/1 liter of water) to a boil, then plunge the celeriac ribbons in and out using tongs or a slotted spoon, transferring them immediately into ice-cold water. Drain well and leave to dry on paper towels, then transfer to a Tupperware container. Pour the cold infused milk into the Tupperware and cover with a lid. Transfer to the fridge for at least 12 hours (ideally overnight).

ROAST THE RED ONIONS

Roast the unpeeled whole onions under the broiler, in a skillet, or in an oven preheated to 350°F/180°C for about 30 to 40 minutes, until completely soft. Cut them down the middle lengthwise and pick out the tender center petals. Transfer 12 of them to a bowl and toss them in a nice red wine vinegar, then season lightly and set aside.

MAKE THE PINE OR ROSEMARY OIL

Place the oil, herbs, and spinach in a small blender or the bowl of a food processor and blend until smooth. Transfer the purée to a saucepan and place over medium heat until it reaches 195°F/90°C, then cook it for about 6 minutes. The oil will split, and the heat helps lock in the color. Strain the oil through a coffee filter into a bowl, then leave to cool and set to one side.

FINISH THE DISH	Melt the butter in a large frying pan until it sizzles and foams, then add the celeriac wedges and fry them in the butter for 5 to 7 minutes, basting them frequently with the butter (using a spoon) so they caramelize all over and take on an even golden color. Remove from the pan and place on paper towels to remove excess butter.

Place the onion petals, celeriac ribbons (drained from the infused milk), and roasted walnuts on a baking sheet and warm through in a low oven.

Place the pan that the celeriac was roasted in back over the heat, then add the broccoli and toss it briefly until warmed through. Remove from the heat.

SERVE	Warm 4 serving bowls. Cut the celeriac wedges in half and arrange some in a serving bowl. Add 2 tablespoons of the hazelnut and chervil dressing. Arrange 3 onion petals, 2 roasted walnuts, 3 broccoli tips, and some chervil leaves in the bowl. In a small pan, combine the crème fraîche with 2 teaspoons of the pine or rosemary oil and heat gently, then spoon into the base of the bowl. Repeat with the remaining 3 plates and serve immediately.

If you have any pine or rosemary oil left over, it freezes well for a month or two.

HOW TO MAKE AN HERB OIL

I love making herb oils. They add a really nice layer of fragrance to salads, sauces, relishes, and finished dishes. They are fun to make and are a great pantry item. For every ¾ cup/200 ml oil (we use grapeseed oil), use 7 ounces/200 g chopped herbs (chives, parsley, cilantro, green onion, basil, or wild garlic) and a pinch of salt. Blend all the ingredients in a high-powered blender or the bowl of a food processor until the mixture is smooth and emulsified. Transfer the blended herbs and oil to a small saucepan over low heat and cook gently, stirring frequently so that it doesn't burn. As you stir, you'll notice the oil particles start separating from the herbs, and the oil will gently start changing color and getting darker. Once the oil has completely separated from the herbs and the small particles of leaves are looking quite dark, remove from the heat, and strain the oil through a very fine cheesecloth or muslin into a bowl set over ice. The dark green oil will keep for up to 2 weeks in the fridge. Add to salads, simple fish, and vegetables.

WOOD-GRILLED CAULIFLOWER HEART

This super-rich and complex main course would satisfy a hungry cowboy during a shortage of meat. Cauliflower heart is one of my favorite "meaty" vegetables. It is amazing what the smoke from a wood-fired grill does to a head of cauliflower if you cook it slowly and baste it regularly. We use the wood-fired grill in the restaurant but you can use a ridged grill pan or gas grill at home.

INGREDIENTS

Serves 4

FOR THE SOUR SPINACH PURÉE:

5 ounces/150 g baby spinach
  leaves, washed
2½ tablespoons table salt
1 ounce/30 g drained sauerkraut
  (squeezed of juice, with juice
  reserved)
2 tablespoons sauerkraut juice
  (from the sauerkraut jar)
Small pinch xanthan gum

FOR THE VADOUVAN SPICE MIX:

4 tablespoons coriander seeds
6 tablespoons cumin seeds
4 teaspoons ground turmeric
1½ teaspoons freshly grated nutmeg
2 teaspoons dried chile flakes
2 teaspoons ground white pepper
4 teaspoons fennel seeds

FOR THE VADOUVAN ONIONS:

3½ tablespoons/50 g unsalted butter,
  cut into cubes
7 ounces/200 g white onions,
  very thinly sliced
Salt
1½ teaspoons vadouvan spice mix

2 large heads cauliflower, outer leaves
  removed and reserved
Maldon sea salt, to season
2 cups/500 ml grapeseed oil, for frying
3½ ounces/100 g fresh curry leaves
7 ounces/200 g blanched almonds
  (skin on)
4 tablespoons crème fraîche
4 button mushrooms, thinly sliced,
  to garnish (optional)
4 brown mushrooms, thinly sliced,
  to garnish (optional)
Grated black truffle, to garnish
  (optional)
24 to 30 sprigs sea purslane, to garnish
  (optional)

MAKE THE SOUR SPINACH PURÉE

Cure the spinach leaves by mixing them in a bowl with the table salt. Rub the leaves with the salt and squeeze until the spinach softens and all the water has been squeezed out. Rinse the spinach under cold running water then squeeze again until it tastes seasoned but not salty. This should take no longer than 5 minutes—if you cure them for too long, the leaves will start to lose their color. Place 2 ounces/60 g of the cured spinach leaves in a blender and add the sauerkraut, sauerkraut juice, and xanthan gum. Blend until smooth, then transfer to a bowl, cover, and chill until needed.

MAKE THE VADOUVAN SPICE MIX

Blend all of the ingredients together in a high-speed blender, spice grinder, or pestle and mortar until coarsely ground. Remove and set aside.

CONTINUED

MAKE THE VADOUVAN
ONIONS

To clarify the butter, put it in a heavy-bottomed saucepan over low heat. As it melts, foam will form on the surface; skim this off with a spoon. You will be left with a clear yellow layer on top and a milky layer underneath. Pour off the clarified fat into a heatproof bowl and discard the milky layer.

Heat most of the clarified butter in a clean saucepan (keeping some back for cooking the cauliflower), add the onions with a pinch of salt, and cook over low heat for about 25 minutes, until golden. Add the spice mix and cook for a few minutes, until the spices are fragrant and toasted. Adjust the seasoning with salt and remove from the heat. Keep warm while you grill the cauliflower.

GRILL THE
CAULIFLOWER

Cut the cauliflowers flat at the root and cut each head in quarters, then each quarter in half to make large chunks.

Burn the wood in your grill until you have a nice bed of glowing embers. Add the cauliflower to the grill and sear it very quickly on both sides, directly over the heat. Rake some of the embers to one side and move the cauliflower chunks onto the side with less heat. Baste them with the remaining clarified butter, season with sea salt, and let them cook slowly. Occasionally move the cauliflower back on the hot part of the grill until it has a nice char on the outside, then move back, baste, and season again. Cook for 15 to 20 minutes, until golden brown and cooked all the way through.

If you don't have a wood-fired grill, cook the cauliflower chunks for about 15 minutes in a ridged grill pan or skillet over high heat, with a stainless steel bowl covering them to make a dome (which will fill with smoke and steam). Lift off the bowl occasionally and brush the cauliflower with butter and season with salt, but try not to remove the bowl too often or all the smoke will dissipate.

FRY THE CURRY LEAVES
& THE ALMONDS

Heat the grapeseed oil in a saucepan and fry the curry leaves in the hot oil for about 40 seconds, until crispy. Remove with a slotted spoon and transfer to a wire rack. Use the same oil to fry the almonds for about 2 minutes, until golden.

SERVE

Heat the sour spinach purée in a pan then place 2 tablespoons on a shallow plate. Place chunks of cauliflower on top, then spoon over some onion mixture. Add dots of crème fraîche around the plate. Sprinkle with toasted almonds and fried curry leaves, adding sliced mushrooms, a couple of gratings of black truffle, and sea purslane sprigs, if using. Repeat for the remaining servings. Serve immediately.

SEARED BEEF SALAD

One of the many exciting challenges of a project like ours at the Firehouse is to create a menu concept that evolves throughout the day, from breakfast, brunch, and lunch through to dinner. We are also a neighborhood restaurant, with regulars who dine several times a week, so our breakfast and lunch menus need to have healthy and tasty dishes that can tempt them. This salad is one of the favorites on our lunch menu. The inspiration for the dish came from the lovely modern Thai restaurants I discovered during my time in San Francisco.

INGREDIENTS

Serves 4

FOR THE FRIED FENNEL:

Grapeseed oil, for deep-frying
1 fennel bulb, outer layers removed
  and base trimmed
1¼ cups/200 g rice flour
Maldon sea salt and freshly ground
  black pepper, to season

FOR THE STEAK MARINADE:

2 teaspoons hon dashi
½ cup/125 ml water
½ cup/125 ml mirin
2½ tablespoons low-salt soy sauce
2 teaspoons toasted sesame oil
1 teaspoon rice vinegar
2 teaspoons fish sauce
Juice of ¼ lemon
½ red chile, seeded and thinly sliced
½ ounce/12 g fresh ginger, peeled and
  thinly sliced

About 1½ pounds/650 g Galician
  Solomillo sirloin (in one piece),
  or other high-quality sirloin

FOR THE CARROT DRESSING:

½ cup/125 ml grapeseed oil
½ ounce/15 g garlic cloves,
  finely chopped
1 ounce/30 g red chiles, finely chopped
5½ ounces/160 g grated carrot
1 tablespoon fish sauce
2 tablespoons extra virgin olive oil
Juice of 1 lime

FOR THE SALAD:

2 fennel bulbs, outer layers removed,
  base trimmed, and bulb thinly shaved
14 ounces/400 g sugar snap peas,
  topped and tailed
11 ounces/320 g arugula, washed
5½ ounces/160 g watercress
7 ounces/200 g green onions, half
  thinly sliced, half charred on a grill
  or grill pan, then chopped
1 cucumber, shaved into thin slices
¾ ounce/20 g mint, leaves picked
¾ ounce/20 g basil, leaves picked
¾ ounce/20 g cilantro, leaves picked

CONTINUED

FRY THE FENNEL

Place the oil in a deep saucepan and heat until it reaches 355°F/180°C. Shave the fennel into very thin slices with a mandoline. Dust generously with rice flour, then remove the excess flour and deep-fry for 3 minutes, until crispy and golden brown. Remove from the oil with a slotted spoon, drain on paper towels, and season well with salt and pepper. Set aside until ready to serve.

MAKE THE STEAK MARINADE

Pour the hon dashi, water, mirin, and soy sauce into a saucepan and place over low heat. Bring to a boil and simmer for about 10 minutes, until it has reduced by a third. Remove from the heat and whisk in the sesame oil, vinegar, fish sauce, and lemon juice. Add the sliced chiles and ginger and blend until smooth with a stick blender.

MARINATE THE BEEF

Keep half the marinade aside for dressing the salad. Place the beef in the remaining marinade for 45 minutes to 2 hours.

MAKE THE CARROT DRESSING

Heat the grapeseed oil in a frying pan over low heat, add the garlic, and fry until fragrant but not browned. Pour the garlic oil through a fine-mesh sieve into a heat-proof bowl, then return the oil to the frying pan, add the chiles and fry for about 2 minutes, until fragrant. Remove from the heat, add the grated carrot, and toss it in the fragrant oil until softened. Transfer the fragrant grated carrot to a bowl and add the fish sauce, olive oil, and lime juice. Set aside at room temperature, uncovered.

COOK THE BEEF

Drain the beef from its marinade (discarding the marinade). Place a frying pan over high heat and sear the beef briefly on all sides until it is covered with a nice crust but is still rare on the inside. Put the beef into the remaining marinade while it rests, then cut it into thin slices just before serving, reserving the remaining marinade to dress the salad. The beef should be raw in the middle and juicy.

SERVE

Mix all the salad ingredients (except the herbs) together with the beef. Toss generous amounts of carrot dressing and steak marinade through the salad and garnish with the crispy fennel and fresh herbs on top. Serve in a big bowl and everyone can dig in.

ROAST CHICKEN SALAD

After construction of the hotel was finished, we spent almost a whole month testing recipes for our opening Firehouse menu. It was an exciting month, and we tested over 500 dishes. One of the dishes was a take on Waldorf salad, made with lobster. We were all very happy with it so gave it to André to try. Because it was a new dish, I described it to him as a lobster Waldorf salad. "Why did you make a salad named after another hotel?" André said. I felt pretty stupid, but saw the funny side. He had a point. So we abandoned that idea and instead created this salad, the Firehouse Roast Chicken Salad. It is very nice, it is American-inspired, and it's ours!

You will have more mayonnaise than you need for this dish, but it keeps well in the fridge for up to 2 days and is delicious with fries or chips.

INGREDIENTS

Serves 4

FOR THE HOUSE DRESSING:

¼ cup/60 ml white soy sauce or
  light soy sauce
¼ cup/60 ml good-quality sherry
  vinegar (red wine, balsamic, cider, or
  champagne vinegar work well, too,
  or freshly squeezed citrus juice)
½ cup/125 ml extra virgin olive oil,
  canola oil, or grapeseed oil
Maldon sea salt and freshly ground
  black pepper, to taste

FOR THE ROAST CHICKEN:

3¼-pound/1.5-kg whole chicken
Maldon sea salt and freshly ground
  black pepper
Juice of 1 lemon, to season
1 bay leaf
4 sprigs rosemary
4 sprigs thyme
4 sprigs flat-leaf parsley
4 tablespoons grapeseed oil
6 tablespoons/85 g unsalted butter

FOR THE CHICKEN FAT MAYONNAISE:

3 free-range egg yolks
1 tablespoon Chardonnay vinegar
  (we use the Forum brand) or white
  balsamic—you need a sweet and floral
  vinegar that isn't too strong or acidic
1 tablespoon Dijon mustard
½ teaspoon Maldon sea salt
1 teaspoon Hennessy Cognac
7 ounces/200 g chicken fat (ask your
  butcher for this, or use duck fat), melted
1 ounce/30 g chervil, finely chopped

FOR THE SALAD:

9 ounces/250 g walnuts
Roast chicken meat
1 bunch green grapes
  (about 5 per person), halved
1 green apple, peeled, cored, chopped
  and placed in a bowl with apple and
  lemon juice to prevent oxidization
2 heads Belgian endive, outer leaves
  removed and tender leaves separated
¾ ounce/20 g tarragon, leaves torn
¾ ounce/20 g chervil, leaves torn
14 ounces/400 g crispy chicken skin
  (see technique on page 116)
4 tablespoons House Dressing,
  or to taste
7 ounces/200 g celeriac ribbons
  (see technique on page 182; optional)

CONTINUED

MAKE THE HOUSE DRESSING	Combine all the ingredients and mix with a fork (don't whisk the dressing, as you want to keep the oil and other liquids separate), season well, and set to one side.

COOK THE WALNUTS	Preheat the oven to 325°F/160°C. Salt the walnuts in a 3 percent salt to 97 percent water solution for 45 minutes. Drain the walnuts and dry them before baking for 8 to 10 minutes. Remove from the oven and cool before serving.

ROAST THE CHICKEN	Truss the chicken and season the cavity with salt, pepper, and lemon juice, then stuff it with the bay leaf, rosemary, thyme, and parsley. Season the outside of the chicken generously with salt and pepper.
	Heat the grapeseed oil in a large frying pan over high heat, then sear the chicken evenly on all sides. Once seared, drain off the oil, then add the butter. Once it has melted and started to foam, baste the chicken all over with the butter, taking care not to let the butter burn. You want a golden brown caramelized crust to the skin, but the chicken should still be quite raw inside.
	Place the seared chicken on a rack over a roasting pan, transfer to the oven, and roast for 30 to 45 minutes, turning the chicken frequently, until the thickest part of the thigh reaches an internal temperature of maximum 150°F/65°C on a probe thermometer. You can take the chicken out of the oven once it reaches an internal temperature of 140°F/60°C and leave it to rest uncovered—the chicken will continue to cook and the residual heat will increase the internal temperature to 150°F/65°C.
	Once the chicken is cool enough to handle, strip off the meat and keep it warm while you make the mayonnaise.

MAKE THE MAYONNAISE	Put all the ingredients except the warm, melted chicken fat and chervil in a blender or the bowl of a food processor and blend until the mixture starts to thicken. Gradually add the chicken fat as you would oil, until all the fat is incorporated and you have a smooth emulsion. Fold in the chopped chervil, cover, and chill.

SERVE	Chill 4 serving plates. Toss all of the salad ingredients together in a bowl except for the mayonnaise. Put a few tablespoons of mayonnaise onto each chilled plate, add the salad, then drizzle more mayonnaise over the salad.

WILD SEA BASS WITH PISTACHIO AND ROMANESCO

This super-tasty dish started out with my love for wood-roasted romanesco broccoli paired with crushed toasted pistachios. These two fantastic ingredients work incredibly well together. The pistachio sauce and finely chopped romanesco with toasted pistachio round off this fish dish perfectly and make an amazing vegetarian dish in their own right, hot or cold (with the omission of the fish sauce in the pistachio sauce, and fish stock replaced with vegetable stock), or a perfect accompaniment for a well-cured sea bass fillet, perfectly cooked so that you can still see the rainbow on the flesh of the fish.

INGREDIENTS

Serves 4

FOR THE PISTACHIO SAUCE:

¾ cup/200 ml fish stock
3 ounces/80 g pistachios
3 tablespoons virgin pistachio oil
7 teaspoons gomme syrup
5 teaspoons fish sauce

FOR THE CHOPPED ROMANESCO:

3 ounces/80 g pistachios
5½ ounces/160 g romanesco
Pinch Maldon sea salt

FOR THE ROASTED ROMANESCO:

1 head romanesco, large stalks removed and florets broken into golf ball–sized pieces
1 tablespoon extra virgin olive oil
Maldon sea salt and freshly ground black pepper

4 (5 ounce/150 g) skin-on sea bass fillets (wild if you can)
Grapeseed oil, for frying
1 heaping tablespoon unsalted butter, for frying
Virgin pistachio oil, for drizzling

MAKE THE PISTACHIO SAUCE

Blend all ingredients together in a blender or the bowl of a food processor until smooth, then pass through a fine-mesh sieve and set aside. Chill until ready to serve.

MAKE THE CHOPPED ROMANESCO

Preheat the oven to 325°F/160°C. Spread the pistachios out on a baking sheet, roast for 8 minutes, until toasted and fragrant, then remove from the oven and leave to cool (leaving the oven on). While the pistachios are cooling, finely chop the romanesco. Chop the roasted pistachios to the same size as the romanesco, add to the romanesco, season with salt, and chill until ready to serve.

ROAST THE ROMANESCO

Toss the romanesco pieces in the olive oil and season with salt and pepper. Transfer to a roasting pan and roast for 15 to 20 minutes, until tender but still a little crunchy. Remove from the oven, adjust seasoning to taste, and set aside somewhere warm until ready to serve.

CONTINUED

COOK THE SEA BASS

Twenty minutes before cooking, let the fish come to room temperature.

Heat a thick layer of grapeseed oil in a large nonstick frying pan. Once hot, put a fillet in the pan, skin side down. Press gently on the fish and it will naturally curl up, then relax. Once relaxed, add the next fish fillet to the pan and repeat until all 4 pieces are cooking.

Reduce the heat and cook the fish for 3 minutes, then rotate each piece of fish 180 degrees, pressing the fish into the pan slightly to make sure it's evenly cooked. Once it is two-thirds cooked (not yet cooked through), increase the heat to medium-high, add the butter, flip the fish over so it's frying skin side up, and baste the fish skin, allowing the butter to brown a little in the pan. Remove from the heat and leave to rest on a warm baking sheet to allow it to cook through.

SERVE

Warm 4 plates. Spoon 1 generous tablespoon of pistachio sauce onto each plate. Lay a piece of fish on the sauce, skin side up, and scatter over the roasted romanesco, then top with chopped romanesco. Finish with a few drops of pistachio oil.

SLOW-COOKED COD, RAW AND ROASTED CARROTS, AND BROWN BUTTER

Cod and carrots is a simple dish with simple ingredients, yet preparing them in an interesting way elevates this to something truly special. The cod is first cured, then made slowly into confit in the oven, and these are both techniques that you can easily replicate at home (providing you have an oven that can be set at a very low temperature) and you can use them on many other fish.

I strongly recommend making this dish when heritage carrots are in season and abundant in your local markets.

INGREDIENTS

Serves 4

1¾ pounds/800 g boneless, skinless cod fillets, cured (see page 106)
⅞ cup/200 g salted butter
8 tablespoons/120 ml Normandy cream or good-quality light cream, seasoned with Maldon sea salt
Red, purple, and white small heritage carrots (1 of each color), shaved very thinly
20 nasturtium leaves
Maldon sea salt and freshly ground black pepper

FOR THE ROAST CARROTS:

4 large purple heritage carrots
Maldon sea salt and freshly ground black pepper
1 bay leaf
4 sprigs thyme
1 tablespoon extra virgin olive oil

FOR THE CONFIT:

1 cup/250 ml extra virgin olive oil
1 cup/250 ml grapeseed oil
2 cloves garlic, bashed
2 bay leaves
4 sprigs thyme

ROAST THE CARROTS

Preheat the oven to 325°F/160°C. Place the 4 purple carrots on a large piece of foil on a baking sheet, season with salt and pepper, and add the bay leaf, thyme, and olive oil. Enclose the carrots in the foil, sealing to form a parcel, and roast in the oven for 25 to 30 minutes, until very soft. Remove from the oven (leaving the oven on) and let them cool at room temperature (still in the foil). Once cool, cut them into pieces, transfer them to a bowl, and mash them roughly. Set aside and keep warm.

MAKE THE BROWN BUTTER

Melt the salted butter in a saucepan over medium-low heat and cook it for about 5 minutes, whisking continuously, until brown, nutty, and fragrant, making sure it doesn't burn. Once it is brown and the bubbles and foam start to disappear, remove the pan from the heat and transfer the butter to a separate, cool, heatproof container (ideally sitting in ice-cold water, to stop the butter cooking), being sure to keep the milk solids with the browned butter.

COOK THE COD

Rinse the cure off the cod fillets, pat them dry, and let them come to room temperature. Mix all of the ingredients for the confit together and add them to a saucepan. Place over medium-low heat until the oil starts simmering, then remove from the heat.

Reduce the oven temperature to 200°F/100°C, or its lowest temperature. Put the cooled oil in a deep roasting pan in the oven. As soon as the oil reaches 150°F/65°C on a probe thermometer, gently drop the cod fillets into the oil and return the tray to the oven for 20 minutes, until the fish starts flaking nicely—it will start to lose its translucency. Remove the tray from the oven and set to one side, keeping the fish fillets in the oil.

SERVE

Warm 4 plates. Spoon 4 tablespoons of mashed carrot onto each plate and place a cod fillet on top. Spoon 2 tablespoons of brown butter over each portion of cod, making sure that brown butter stays warm (if it gets cold, it congeals). Spoon 2 tablespoons of cream onto each serving, scatter carrot shavings around the plates, and garnish with nasturtium leaves (5 per plate). Serve immediately.

MAPLE-GLAZED SMOKED SALMON, KOHLRABI RIBBONS, AND SMOKED BROTH

During my travels around North America, I fell in love with the combination of lightly smoked slow-cooked salmon with maple syrup. This maple glaze works beautifully with the flavor of the salmon and the smoked broth. We use smoked eel bones to make the broth because they work brilliantly and we happen to have them in our kitchen, but if you don't have a pile of eel bones taking up space in your fridge, use smoked salmon bones, smoked salmon trimmings, or smoked salmon skin instead.

If you can't buy salmon skin, cook the salmon fillets with their skin on and remove the skin before serving, then crisp them up on both sides in a nonstick pan.

<table>
<tr><td>INGREDIENTS</td><td colspan="2">Serves 4</td></tr>
<tr><td></td><td>

1 kohlrabi, halved lengthwise, then each piece halved horizontally and sliced into thin 4-inch/10-cm lengths or long shavings with a mandoline
About 1½ pounds/650 g salmon fillets, cured (see page 106)
Succulent foraged herbs (we use sea purslane, samphire, and stonecrop—a handful of each)
Dill, to garnish
Extra virgin olive oil, to serve

FOR THE BUTTERMILK & EEL STOCK (SMOKED BROTH):

3⅔ cups/820 ml buttermilk
4 ounces/125 g smoked eel trimmings and bones (store-bought) or smoked salmon trimmings and/or bones
2 teaspoons table salt

FOR THE CURED SALMON CAVIAR:

1¾ ounces/50 g salmon caviar (also called roe)
1 teaspoon white soy sauce
1½ teaspoons superfine sugar
½ cup/100 g dashi

</td><td>

FOR THE KOMBU:

½ ounce/15 g wild royal kombu, leaves broken into pieces
1¾ cups/400 ml water
1 teaspoon shiro dashi
⅙ ounce/5 g fresh ginger, skin scraped off with spoon and root sliced

FOR THE SALMON GLAZE:

2½ tablespoons unsalted butter
1 tablespoon maple syrup
2 tablespoons water
2 teaspoons chipotle paste

FOR THE CRISPY SALMON SKINS:

14 ounces/400 g salmon skin, scaled (from the fishmonger)
2 cups/500 ml grapeseed oil, for deep-frying
Fine sea salt, for sprinkling

</td></tr>
<tr><td>MAKE THE BUTTERMILK & EEL STOCK</td><td colspan="2">

Put the buttermilk and smoked eel or salmon trimmings in a saucepan and bring to a boil. Keep at a rolling boil for about 5 minutes, until the buttermilk splits, then remove from the heat, season with the salt, and transfer to a heatproof container. Cover and leave to cool down until it reaches room temperature. Strain through a double layer of muslin into a clean pan and set aside. Discard the curds.

</td></tr>
</table>

CONTINUED

CURE THE SALMON CAVIAR

Remove the caviar from the jar and rinse in a sieve under cold running water. Transfer to a bowl and add the white soy sauce, sugar, and dashi. Chill for about 45 minutes, until the roe hardens and is nice and crunchy. Strain through a sieve and chill the caviar until ready to serve.

MAKE THE KOMBU

Place all the ingredients in a large saucepan over medium heat, mix gently, and bring to a boil, then reduce the heat and simmer gently for 20 to 25 minutes, until the kombu is tender. Strain and reserve the kombu leaves until you are ready to serve.

PREPARE THE KOHLRABI

Gently toss the kohlrabi strips in 1 to 2 tablespoons of the warm buttermilk and eel stock and set aside.

MAKE THE SALMON GLAZE

Melt the butter gently in a saucepan and continue to heat until browned (see page 202 for brown butter method). Remove from the heat and set aside until it reaches room temperature. Add the maple syrup and water, return the pan to low heat, and simmer for about 5 minutes, until reduced, emulsified, and thick enough to coat the back of a spoon. Add the chipotle paste to the maple glaze. Set the glaze aside.

MAKE THE CRIPSY SALMON SKIN

Preheat the oven to 200°F/100°C, or its lowest temperature. Line a baking sheet with parchment paper, then spray the paper with oil to prevent the skin sticking. Place the skin on the parchment, well spaced out and flat. Bake for 15 to 20 minutes, until dry but not colored. Remove from the oven (leaving the oven on for cooking the salmon) and set aside to cool. Meanwhile, heat the grapeseed oil in a deep-fat fryer or deep saucepan. Fry the dry skin in batches for 30 to 40 seconds, until it puffs up. Remove from the oil with a slotted spoon and leave to drain on paper towels, seasoning immediately with salt. Keep in a warm place until ready to serve.

COOK THE SALMON

Remove the salmon from the fridge and let it reach room temperature. Rinse the cure off the salmon fillets and pat them dry with paper towels. Remove the skin (reserving it for frying, if you haven't been able to source separate salmon skin—see recipe introduction). Heat a frying pan over high heat, then sear the salmon, one fillet at a time, on what was the skin side for 1 minute, until crispy on the outside but still raw inside. Remove from the heat, transfer to a baking sheet lined with parchment paper, and bake in the oven (it should still be set at 200°F/100°C) for 8 to 10 minutes, until the internal temperature of the salmon on a probe thermometer is 120°F/50°C. Start checking the internal temperature after 5 minutes. Remove the salmon from the oven, brush it generously with the glaze, and sprinkle with a little salt.

SERVE   Warm 4 plates. Place warm kohlrabi strips and kombu on a plate. Spoon a tablespoon of cured roe on top and place the salmon on the plate. Top with the crispy skin and scatter over a handful of the herbs. Add a couple of dill fronds and a generous tablespoon of olive oil. Gently warm through the smoked eel or salmon broth and spoon the broth on the plate. Plate the remaining servings and serve immediately.

MONKFISH COOKED OVER PINE, PUFFED BARLEY, AND FENNEL

This was one of the original Firehouse dishes, along with the Crab Doughnuts (see page 75).

Menu development and tastings for the Firehouse started almost ten months before we opened our doors, back in summer 2013, and they gave me a chance to reminisce about my days in North America and the flavors I brought back with me.

Big North American cities are cultural melting pots, which makes the food scene particularly exciting. Far-flung ingredients such as chipotle chiles, miso paste, and umeboshi are commonplace in many of the cities' kitchens and emerge on menus in new and exciting ways. This dish was one of the first that I felt most strongly evoked my passage through North America: the fish, the eclectic list of ingredients, the cooking techniques, and the creative approach all capture the spirit of what modern North American cuisine is about.

INGREDIENTS

Serves 4

FOR THE BARLEY MISO:

1¾ cups/400 ml water
1⁄14 ounce/2 g Maldon sea salt
½ cup/100 g barley
⅓ cup/100 g apple purée (see page 102)
1 tablespoon white miso paste
  (light miso)
1⁄14 ounce/2 g preserved lemon rind,
  thinly chopped
¾ ounce/20 g fennel, thinly diced and
  blanched for 2 minutes in salted water
Squeeze fresh lemon juice
1 tablespoon chive oil (see page 183)

FOR THE ROASTED FENNEL:

2 fennel bulbs, trimmed
Maldon sea salt, to season
Extra virgin olive oil, to season

FOR THE FENNEL PURÉE:

1 tablespoon unsalted butter
1 tablespoon grapeseed oil
2 fennel bulbs, very thinly sliced
1 green apple
1 teaspoon white miso paste
  (light miso)
Juice of ½ lemon
Maldon sea salt, to season
1 teaspoon sugar or honey (optional)

FOR THE MONKFISH:

1⅓ pounds/640 g monkfish loin fillet
  (1 fillet)
Maldon sea salt, to season
2 tablespoons grapeseed oil, plus extra
  for frying the barley, if using
2 tablespoons unsalted butter
7 ounces/200 g pine needles
  (or rosemary if you can't get hold
  of pine)

TO SERVE:

⅓ ounce/10 g stonecrop or other
  beach-foraged herb such as sea
  purslane

CONTINUED

MAKE THE BARLEY MISO

Bring the water to a boil, add the salt, then add the barley. Cook until tender, then drain and leave to cool. Combine all the ingredients (setting aside ¼ cup/50 g of the barley for frying to garnish, if using) and mix well. Adjust seasoning if necessary, and chill until needed.

MAKE THE ROASTED FENNEL

Preheat the oven to 325°F/160°C. Season the fennel bulbs with salt and drizzle with extra virgin olive oil then wrap them in foil. Place the foil parcels on a baking sheet and bake in the oven for 15 to 20 minutes, until tender. Remove the fennel from the foil, making sure you save any juices. Cut the bulbs into quarters, reseason with salt, spoon or brush over the reserved juices, and keep warm until ready to serve.

MAKE THE FENNEL PURÉE

Heat the butter and grapeseed oil in a frying pan over low heat, add the sliced fennel and sweat gently for 6 to 7 minutes (so that the fennel doesn't caramelize or burn) until it is very soft. Grate the apple into the mix, skin and all, discarding the core. Continue cooking until the apple is soft, adding a little water if necessary, then remove from the heat and blend until smooth. Season with the miso, lemon juice, and salt to taste. There should be enough natural sweetness from the fennel and apple, if they have been cooked slowly enough, but if you need to sweeten the purée, add 1 teaspoon of sugar or honey. Set aside at room temperature until ready to serve.

COOK THE MONKFISH

Set the oven to its lowest temperature (about 150°F/65°C maximum). Cut the fish into 4 portions. Season generously with salt just before cooking. Heat the grapeseed oil in a frying pan and sear the monkfish on all sides until golden brown. Add the butter to the pan. Baste the fish with the foaming butter then remove from the heat.

Place a wire rack over a large roasting pan and add a layer of pine needles to cover the bottom of the pan. Carefully set the needles alight with a blowtorch and, just as it starts catching, place the monkfish on the wire rack. Cover loosely with foil so the fire stops and the pine smokes. Put the covered pan in the oven and cook for 8 minutes until the internal temperature of the fish reaches 140°F/60°C on a probe thermometer. Remove from the oven and let it rest, then remove the foil just before serving.

FRY THE PUFFED BARLEY GARNISH (OPTIONAL)

Heat some grapeseed oil in a frying pan, add the reserved, cooked barley and fry briefly until it puffs up. Drain on paper towels.

SERVE

Warm 4 plates. Place 2 tablespoons of fennel purée on each plate. Cut the monkfish fillets into 2 pieces, season with salt, and place next to the purée. Spoon a generous 2 teaspoons of barley miso onto the side of each plate. Add 2 pieces of roasted fennel and scatter with a handful of beach herbs and some puffed barley, if using.

RED MULLET, ENDIVE HEARTS, MUSSELS, AND MARCONA ALMONDS

Red mullet is one of my favorite fish. I remember prepping some for a cooking demo in Portugal, and they had been out of the water for less than four hours. They were one of the sweetest fish I had ever tasted. When fish is this fresh and firm, I like to just cut off a small piece of flesh and eat it raw, maybe with a dash of good-quality olive oil and a sprinkling of flaked sea salt. Please try this: it gives you an awareness of the flavor that will help you find ways of serving it that preserve the flavor you discovered in that raw bite. If you cannot source red mullet, substitute snapper or sea bass.

The garnishes in this dish showcase the components that make up the original profile flavor of the fish.

INGREDIENTS

Serves 4

2 heads Belgian endive, quartered, outer leaves removed and reserved
2 tablespoons canola oil
2 tablespoons white soy sauce or shiro dashi
17 ounces/500 g mussels, rinsed, scrubbed clean, and bearded (discard any with broken shells, or whose shells don't close when tapped)
2 tablespoons extra virgin olive oil

Squeeze fresh lemon juice
4 red mullet (about 1¾ pounds/ 800 g total), gutted, scaled, filleted, pin-boned, and cured (see page 106)
Grapeseed oil, for drizzling
Toasted Marcona or regular almonds, coarsely chopped (about 16 almonds per person)
Small bunch dill
Grated zest of 1 orange (optional)

PREPARE THE CHICORY

Put the quartered endive hearts in a sealable bag, drizzle with the canola oil, and season with white soy sauce or shiro dashi. Seal and transfer it to the fridge for 2 hours.

MAKE THE MUSSEL STOCK

Preheat the oven to 325°F/160°C. Put the mussels on a baking sheet and cover with foil. Bake for 8 minutes, or until their shells open. Remove the mussels from the oven and let them cool. Strain the juices into a bowl and reserve. Pick the mussels out of their shells (discard any that remain closed) and add them to the reserved juices. Add the olive oil and lemon juice, mix together, and set aside.

SEAR THE RED MULLET

Rinse the cure off the red mullet and pat dry with paper towels. Brush the fish skin with grapeseed oil and heat a frying pan until very hot. Sear the fish skin side down in batches for 30 seconds, then immediately remove from the heat.

SERVE

Warm 4 plates. Place 2 red mullet fillets on each plate, add the endive hearts and reserved outer leaves. Spoon over the mussels with mussel stock, scatter with the toasted almonds, dill, and orange zest. Finish with a generous drizzle of grapeseed oil.

TURBOT WITH SEAWEED HOLLANDAISE

Because of the high volume of guests we serve at the Firehouse every day, we need to capture a very wide audience. Some guests visit us because they have heard so much about the place; others visit us for the food and wine. As a result we need to keep our menus adventurous to a degree, but also comforting and nurturing, to appeal to all. This simple turbot dish appeals to guests who just want to eat something tasty that is not too adventurous; a "Tuesday" dish.

You can make the seaweed butter in advance. It keeps—well wrapped—in the fridge for at least a week, and in the freezer for up to 6 months.

INGREDIENTS

Serves 4

FOR THE SEAWEED BUTTER:

3½ ounces/100 g dried dulse
3½ ounces/100 g dried kombu
1½ pounds/700 g unsalted butter,
  at room temperature

FOR THE SEAWEED HOLLANDAISE:

4 tablespoons seaweed butter
2½ tablespoons white wine vinegar
½ shallot, thinly diced
1 free-range egg yolk
Freshly squeezed lemon juice, to taste
Pinch Maldon sea salt

17 ounces/500 g Jersey Royal potatoes
  (or other small new potatoes)
3½ ounces/100 g dried kombu,
  thinly chopped
1⅓ pounds/600 g sea kale or regular
  kale, washed and trimmed (thick
  stalks removed)
Extra virgin olive oil, for drizzling
1¾ pounds/800 g skin-on turbot fillets,
  pin-boned and cured (see page 106)
Grapeseed oil, for frying
Maldon sea salt
Mustard flowers, to serve (optional)

MAKE THE SEAWEED
BUTTER

Place the dulse and kombu in a food processor and blend until they form fine crumbs. Transfer to a bowl, add the butter, and beat to combine. Leave at room temperature for a few hours. If you're making it in advance, wrap it in plastic wrap and chill or freeze until needed.

MAKE THE SEAWEED
HOLLANDAISE

Melt the 4 tablespoons of seaweed butter and set aside. Put the vinegar and shallot in a small saucepan and place over low heat. Slowly bring to a boil, then simmer for 5 minutes until reduced. Strain into a heat-proof bowl. Whisk the egg yolk and 1 teaspoon of the strained vinegar and shallot reduction in a heatproof bowl over a pan of simmering water, making sure the bottom of the bowl doesn't touch the water, until it thickens. Slowly drizzle in the melted seaweed butter, whisking continuously, to emulsify, then remove from the heat and season to taste with lemon juice and salt. Cover the surface of the hollandaise with plastic wrap, to prevent a skin forming, and leave somewhere warm (it can't be reheated before serving).

CONTINUED

COOK THE POTATOES

Cook the potatoes in a saucepan of boiling salted water along with the kombu for 10 to 15 minutes until the potatoes are tender. Drain most of the liquid through a sieve, reserving 5 tablespoons/70 ml, and being careful not to break up the potatoes. Leave the drained potatoes and kombu to cool down at room temperature.

Once cool, crush the potatoes gently with a fork, leaving them quite chunky (or quarter them). Transfer them to a saucepan, along with the kombu they were cooked with, and 5 tablespoons/70 ml of the reserved cooking liquid. Cook over low heat for 5 minutes. Add 2 tablespoons of the seaweed butter and stir constantly over low heat for a further 2 minutes, until the butter melts and the sauce emulsifies and thickens. Remove from the heat and set aside.

COOK THE KALE

Blanch the kale leaves in boiling salted water for 4 minutes until tender. Drain and refresh in ice-cold water if not serving immediately. Toss with olive oil and sprinkle with a little salt.

COOK THE TURBOT

Preheat the oven to 100°F/45°C, or as low as it will go. Rinse the cure off the fish and pat it dry with paper towels. Heat a frying pan until hot, add a drizzle of grapeseed oil, and sear the turbot in batches, skin side down, for 30 seconds. Transfer the seared turbot to a roasting pan (or keep it in the frying pan if the pan is ovenproof) and bake in the oven for 8 to 10 minutes, until the internal temperature reaches 100°F/45°C on a probe thermometer (a toothpick inserted gently into the flesh should meet a little resistance, and not go smoothly all the way through the flesh). Remove the turbot from the oven and sear it again, skin side down, in a hot frying pan with a little more grapeseed oil. Remove the fish from the pan and let it rest on a cool, clean chopping board for 1 to 2 minutes.

SERVE

Divide the potatoes between 4 warm plates. Drizzle over 1 tablespoon of the seaweed hollandaise, then place the fish on the plate. Garnish with the blanched sea kale and mustard flowers, sprinkle with a little salt, and serve immediately.

ROASTED CHICKEN, KALE, AND BREAD PUDDING

Roast chicken and stuffing reminds me of my first years living in North America. In Miami there was a chain of restaurants that specialized in roast chicken, and stuffing was one of the side dishes. Since I had little money at the time and didn't have a car, I would go to wherever my friends who drove picked, and this chain was a popular choice. They always seemed more interested in smoking and getting high than finding a good local spot to eat. My memories of those days are marred by some of the worst food experiences in my life! This chicken dish was created to please our diners but also to replace the memory of that bad roast chicken and stuffing with something tasty and exciting that will put a smile on your face.

Serves 4

INGREDIENTS

2 very small corn-fed chickens
  (1⅔ pounds/750 g each), trussed
  (you can ask your butcher to do this)
Hay, to stuff the chickens (organic,
  from a pet shop)
1 tablespoon grapeseed oil
2 tablespoons unsalted butter

FOR THE MUSHROOM PURÉE:

2 tablespoons golden raisins
2 tablespoons dried cranberries
7 tablespoons/100 ml water
3 tablespoons unsalted butter
1 small shallot
1 clove garlic, chopped
⅓ teaspoon Maldon sea salt,
  plus more to taste
4½ tablespoons/65 ml port
2 tablespoons brandy
1 tablespoon grapeseed oil, for frying
9 ounces/250 g shiitake mushrooms

FOR THE BREAD PUDDING:

10 to 12 ounces/300 to 350 g
  brioche, crusts removed, cut
  into ¾-inch/2-cm cubes
1 tablespoon unsalted butter
½ clove garlic, finely chopped
½ shallot, finely chopped
3 ounces/80 g kale, washed and
  trimmed (thick stalks removed)
1¼ cups/300 ml brown chicken stock
6½ tablespoons/95 ml heavy cream
4 free-range egg yolks
1/14 ounce/2 g rosemary leaves,
  thinly chopped
Grated zest of 1 unwaxed lemon
¼ teaspoon table salt

FOR THE KALE:

⅔ cup/150 ml water
Pinch Maldon sea salt
⅞ cup/200 g unsalted butter, cubed
2¼ pounds/1 kg kale, washed and
  trimmed (thick stalks removed)
  and coarsely chopped

MAKE THE MUSHROOM PURÉE

Place the raisins, cranberries, and water in a saucepan and bring to a boil. Remove from the heat, cover the pan with plastic wrap, and set aside for 1 to 2 hours until the raisins and berries have absorbed most of the water and plumped up.

In a separate saucepan, melt 1½ tablespoons of the butter over medium heat. Add the shallot, garlic, and salt. Cook gently for about 10 minutes, until the shallot is soft and almost beginning to caramelize. Add the port and half the brandy and cook for 5 minutes. When the alcohol has reduced, add the soaked raisins and cranberries along with any residual water and continue to cook.

CONTINUED

Meanwhile, heat the grapeseed oil in a large frying pan. When the oil starts smoking, add the shiitake mushrooms, the remaining butter, and the remaining brandy, then add the mushroom mixture to the pan with the reduced alcohol, berries, and shallots. Stir well, then transfer to a blender or food processor and blend on high speed until you have a smooth paste, then pass it through a fine-mesh sieve into a bowl. Adjust the seasoning to taste, cover, and chill for 24 hours to allow the flavors to develop.

PREPARE THE CHICKEN

Stuff the cavities of the chickens with hay and let them sit in the fridge, uncovered, for about 4 hours.

MAKE THE BREAD PUDDING

Preheat the oven to 350°F/170°C and line a baking sheet with parchment paper. Place the brioche cubes on the tray and bake for 8 minutes, until lightly toasted and golden brown. Remove from the oven and set aside to cool.

Melt the butter in a saucepan, add the garlic and shallot, and cook gently over low heat for 5 to 6 minutes, until very soft. Add the kale with a splash of cold water and cook over low heat for about 5 minutes, stirring, until the kale is tender. Remove from the heat, transfer to a bowl, leave to cool, then cover and chill. Once cold, coarsely chop the kale.

Bring the chicken stock to a boil in a pan, then remove from the heat. Stir in the toasted brioche, cream, egg yolks, rosemary, lemon zest, chopped kale, and salt. Adjust the seasoning to taste, leave to cool, then cover and chill until needed.

COOK THE CHICKEN

Place a large nonstick frying pan over high heat, add a drizzle of grapeseed oil, and swirl it around to coat the bottom of the pan. Sear one of the chickens on the crown first then on all sides, until the skin starts to caramelize (but is not burnt or ripped), then add half of the butter. Push the chicken to the top of the pan, then tilt the pan gently toward you until the butter collects in a pool on the side of the pan nearest you and starts foaming. Baste the chicken on all sides with the foaming butter until it is golden brown, being quick so that the butter doesn't burn. Repeat with the other chicken. Transfer the chickens to a wire rack sitting over a roasting pan.

Set your oven to 200°F/100°C, then roast the chicken for about 50 minutes, until the breast side of the leg reaches an internal temperature of 150°F/65°C on a probe thermometer (this makes for a really moist chicken, where the meat fibers have just set, though if you prefer you can cook it for a little longer). Remove the tray from the oven and leave the chicken to rest, uncovered, for about 15 minutes, and reserve some of the juices from the tray. If you don't have a probe thermometer, cook the chicken at a slightly higher temperature, and test that the juices run clear when a sharp knife is inserted into the thickest part of the leg.

COOK THE KALE

While the chicken is resting, bring the water with the pinch of salt to a boil, then add the cubed butter a little at a time, whisking continuously to form an emulsion. Once you have an emulsified liquid, add the kale and cook for 5 minutes over medium heat.

SERVE

Carve the chickens, separating them into breasts, legs, and thighs. If the skin is not super crispy, baste it with a little bit of fat from the roasting pan, then place the chicken under the broiler on the hottest setting for 30 to 60 seconds.

Warm 4 plates. Place 2 tablespoons of mushroom purée on the bottom of each plate. Serve 1 breast, 1 leg, and 1 thigh per person. Spoon a little kale around each plate and serve with individual portions of warm bread pudding on the side.

SPRING LAMB, ROASTED SMOKED CARROTS, BLACK GARLIC, AND GOAT MILK CURD

Spring lamb is hugely celebrated in the UK, and our take on it, pairing aged lamb with black garlic paste, smoked carrots, and goat milk curd, works beautifully.

Aging lamb had been on my mind for a while, and once we'd met Daphne, our small-scale Welsh lamb supplier, we discussed it, as aging lamb meat is not common practice. We started aging saddles, serving the meat at the Firehouse after twenty-one days, and the result was really fantastic. The meat tenses up and loses moisture, and the fat takes on a much stronger flavor. As a result, the meat—while sweet—becomes denser, richer, and stronger in gaminess without becoming as heavy as a mutton. This aging process is tricky to achieve at home, but you could try persuading your butcher to hang it for you: they might be pleasantly surprised, and grateful that you've introduced them to a new idea.

INGREDIENTS

Serves 4

FOR THE GOAT MILK CURD (OPTIONAL):

1 quart/1 liter whole goat milk
1 tablespoon rennet
1 tablespoon freshly squeezed
  lemon juice

FOR THE LAMB JUS:

17 ounces/500 g raw chicken wings
17 ounces/500 g lamb trimmings,
  cut into ¾-inch/2-cm cubes,
  or diced shoulder
½ yellow onion, thickly sliced
1 shallot, thickly sliced
3 cloves garlic, halved
Sprig thyme
2 bay leaves
2 quarts/2 liters water
Maldon sea salt

FOR THE BLACK GARLIC PASTE:

½ ounce/15 g gem heart lettuce
  (about ½ heart)
2 teaspoons unsalted butter, melted
2¼ ounces/65 g black garlic, cloves peeled
⅓ cup/80 ml chicken stock
2 teaspoons Korean chile paste
Tiny pinch xanthan gum
2 teaspoons toasted sesame oil
Maldon sea salt

FOR THE ROAST CARROTS:

6 carrots, with leafy tops intact
1 tablespoon unsalted butter, plus extra
  for reheating (optional)
Maldon sea salt and freshly ground
  black pepper

4 (9-ounce/250-g) pieces lamb
  sirloin (aged if possible), fat scored
  in a criss-cross pattern
4 tablespoons very good-quality
  store-bought or homemade goat
  milk curd
Maldon sea salt

CONTINUED

MAKE THE GOAT MILK CURD (OPTIONAL)

Place the goat milk in a saucepan and heat it until it reaches 170°F/77°C. Remove from the heat, add the rennet and lemon juice, cover, and leave for 1 hour, then strain through cheesecloth over a clean bowl. Chill the curd until ready to serve.

MAKE THE LAMB JUS

Preheat the oven to 400°F/200°C and put a roasting pan in the oven to heat up. Place the chicken wings in the hot pan and roast them for about 15 minutes, until they start to brown. Drain a little fat from the pan, add the cubed lamb trimmings, and put it back in the oven to roast for a further 15 minutes, until the trimmings are browning and starting to caramelize. If you doubt whether the chicken and lamb will brown and caramelize sufficiently in the oven, heat the roasting pan on the stove top and brown the chicken and lamb over medium-high heat before transferring to the oven. Drain the fat from the pan (reserving it to add to the jus later), then add the onion, shallot, garlic, and herbs and roast for a further 15 minutes, until golden brown. Add the water to the hot pan with the other ingredients and bake for 1 hour 20 minutes.

Pass the stock through a sieve into a saucepan and discard the solids. Strain again through a fine-mesh sieve into a clean pan and place over low heat. Simmer for about 45 minutes, until reduced by about a third (or up to a quarter), regularly skimming away any impurities, until you have a flavorful, clear, brown jus. Adjust the seasoning with salt just before serving.

MAKE THE BLACK GARLIC PASTE

Heat a ridged grill pan over a high heat, then add the lettuce heart cut side down to the pan. Season with salt and baste with butter for 10 minutes, until the lettuce is dark brown and charred all over. Transfer to a plate, cover with plastic wrap, and set to one side to steam for about 10 minutes. Remove the plastic wrap and finely chop the lettuce heart. Place the remaining ingredients in a saucepan and bring to a boil. Simmer for 10 minutes, until the garlic is soft, then add the chopped lettuce and blend in a blender or a food processor to form a paste. Chill until ready to serve.

ROAST THE CARROTS

We smoke the carrots in our wood-fired grill for 20 minutes, but roasting them gives an equally satisfying result. Preheat the oven to 325°F/160°C and remove the leafy tops from the carrots (clean them and place them in iced water until ready to serve). Place a roasting pan over high heat. Add the butter, then add the carrots, and fry for 3 to 4 minutes, until they start to caramelize. Season with salt and pepper, then transfer the dish to the oven and roast for 45 minutes. Reduce the oven temperature to its lowest setting and leave the carrots in the oven to keep warm until ready to serve.

COOK THE LAMB

Set the oven to 150°F/65°C or its lowest setting. Heat a frying pan over medium-low heat. Season the lamb steaks with salt, then cook them gently in the pan, one at a time and fat side down, for about 10 minutes. Every now and then, as the fat is rendered into the pan, tilt the pan and spoon the rendered fat over the meat to baste it. Once they are nicely caramelized and the fat is golden brown, place the lamb fat side up on a rack placed over a baking sheet in the oven and cook for 6 to 7 minutes, or until the lamb steaks reach an internal temperature of 120°F/48°C on a probe thermometer. Remove and leave to rest, uncovered, somewhere warm but not too hot, for 8 to 10 minutes, fat side up.

SERVE

Warm 4 bowls. Carve the rested lamb into thick slices and season with sea salt. Place a tablespoon of the black garlic paste on the bottom of each bowl, then add the carrots and 1 tablespoon of goat milk curd. Place the lamb on the side, spoon 2 tablespoons of jus (adding a little of the retained lamb and chicken fat to it, if you like) in the bottom of the bowl (not over the lamb), and sprinkle with fresh carrot tops. Serve immediately.

RIB-EYE STEAK WITH CHIMICHURRI AND LACINATO KALE

The wood-fired grill plays a huge role in our cooking at the Firehouse, and a nice big steak is a real must on a North American menu. This rib-eye, at 14 ounces/400 g, is big by European standards; we chose it not because of its size but because of the aging and the flavor it has when cooked on the wood-fired grill. There are plenty of goodlooking steaks around, but it is hard to find one that is truly amazing, from beef that has been fed well and aged long enough to give it that richness and depth of flavor that we equate to the flavor of a "real steak." For the one hundred or so steaks that we serve daily, we use grass-fed Irish beef (aged for 48 to 60 days). If you are only cooking for four, try sourcing grass-fed rib-eye steak that has been aged for 60 to 80 days. It's expensive, but it will probably be the best steak of your life.

The chimichurri is a tribute to my father, who spent his last days in Nicaragua and taught me there how to make a good chimichurri.

It might just look like a plate of steak, but there are lots of personal emotions in this dish. Perhaps you will be able to taste them.

INGREDIENTS

Serves 4

FOR THE CHIMICHURRI SAUCE:

½ ounce/12 g garlic (about 2 large cloves), finely grated
½ ounce/12 g jalapeño chile (about 1), seeded and finely chopped
½ ounce/12 g horseradish, finely grated
Grated zest and juice of 1 unwaxed lime
½ ounce/12 g cilantro stalks, finely chopped
1⅔ cups/375 ml grapeseed oil
1 ounce/30 g chives, finely snipped
3½ ounces/100 g flat-leaf parsley leaves, finely chopped
2 ounces/60 g cilantro leaves, finely chopped
3 ounces/90 g mint leaves, finely chopped
Maldon sea salt and freshly ground black pepper

FOR THE CHIMICHURRI PURÉE (OPTIONAL):

4 tablespoons grapeseed oil
1 white onion, thinly sliced
2 cloves garlic, thinly sliced
1 jalapeño chile, seeded and finely chopped

Juice of 2 limes, plus more to taste
½ bunch chives, chopped
½ bunch cilantro leaves, chopped
½ bunch flat-leaf parsley leaves, chopped
½ bunch mint leaves, chopped
Maldon sea salt and ground white pepper, to season

FOR THE CONFIT MUSHROOMS:

4 baby portobello or large chestnut mushrooms, brushed and trimmed
Maldon sea salt
1 cup/250 ml extra virgin olive oil, plus extra for drizzling
1 cup/250 ml grapeseed oil
1 head garlic, halved across the middle
1 bay leaf
Large sprig thyme

FOR THE ONION RINGS:

2 cups/500 ml grapeseed oil, for frying
2 white onions, peeled and cut into ½-inch/1-cm-thick rings
1 cup/250 ml buttermilk
1¼ cups/200 g rice flour
Salt and ground white pepper, to season

CONTINUED

FOR THE KALE:	FOR THE RIB-EYE STEAK:

2 tablespoons unsalted butter
1 tablespoon freshly squeezed
  lemon juice
1 tablespoon sherry vinegar
Salt, to season
14 ounces/400 g washed and trimmed
  lacinato kale, thicker stalks removed
  and each leaf halved
	4 (14-ounce/400-g) rib-eye steaks,
	  with a generous amount of fat
	  (ideally dry-aged for at least 48 days),
	  at room temperature
	6 tablespoons/85 g unsalted butter,
	  melted
	Maldon sea salt and freshly ground
	  black pepper

MAKE THE CHIMICHURRI SAUCE

Combine the garlic, chile, horseradish, lime zest and juice, and chopped cilantro stalks in a bowl. Add the grapeseed oil, mix to combine, then add the chopped herbs and season to taste. Set aside at room temperature.

MAKE THE CHIMICHURRI PURÉE (OPTIONAL)

Heat the oil in a saucepan over low heat, add the onion, garlic, and chile and sauté for 6 to 8 minutes, until soft. Season, increase the heat, add the lime juice and herbs, and stir for 2 minutes, until the herbs wilt. Transfer to a blender or the bowl of a food processor and blend to a smooth purée. Adjust the seasoning with pepper, salt, and lime juice and set aside. If making ahead, only add the lime juice when you're ready to serve.

MAKE THE CONFIT MUSHROOMS

Rub the mushrooms with salt for couple of minutes, then let them stand in a bowl or colander for 15 minutes. Quarter each mushroom. Place the olive oil and grapeseed oil in a pan over medium heat, then add the garlic, bay leaf, and thyme. Bring the oil to a simmer then remove from the heat. Add the quartered mushrooms and leave to cool.

MAKE THE ONION RINGS

Heat the grapeseed oil in a deep saucepan until it reaches 355°F/180°C. Separate the onion rings and place the rings in a bowl. Pour the buttermilk into a separate bowl and place the rice flour in another bowl. Season the buttermilk and flour with salt and white pepper. Dip each onion ring into the buttermilk, then dust each ring with flour, dredging them generously in each mix. Fry the rings in batches for 3 to 4 minutes until golden brown and crispy. Drain on paper towels, season with salt, and set aside.

COOK THE KALE

Melt the butter with the lemon juice and sherry vinegar in a shallow saucepan, then increase the heat. Once the sauce starts to emulsify, season it well with salt, and add the kale, turning it for 3 to 4 minutes, until just al dente. Remove from the heat.

COOK THE STEAK

Preheat the oven to 150°F/65°C (or its lowest temperature) and heat a ridged grill pan or barbecue grill until very hot. Sear the steaks on both sides, for 5 to 7 minutes in total, until they take on char marks. Place on a baking sheet, brush with melted butter, and season with salt and pepper. Transfer to the oven for 10 to 25 minutes, until they reach an internal temperature of 110°F/45°C on a probe thermometer. Remove from the oven and set aside.

SERVE

Warm 4 plates. Give the steaks a burst of heat on each side in a hot grill pan if they've cooled, then brush again with butter and season with salt and pepper. Carve them or serve them whole. Plate the steaks, add the chimichurri purée, if using, then spoon the chimichurri sauce over and around the steaks. Remove the mushrooms from the oil, and season them with salt. Place the kale and mushrooms on the plates and drizzle with olive oil. Place the fried onion rings on top and serve immediately.

WHERE THERE'S SMOKE...

THE ALTAR OF THE FIREHOUSE KITCHEN is a commanding adjustable-height wood-burning grill, modeled after an Argentinian *parrilla*. As to its handsomeness, there are no doubters. But in the month between its installation and the restaurant's opening, there were some long days and nights of inquiry as the kitchen team worked to master the fire-breathing behemoth.

LORD OF THE LOGS

First, the billowing clouds of smoke it discharged had a tendency to infiltrate every corner of the hotel, setting off the fire alarms. The second, more intractable problem was that for all the fire and smoke, the food cooked on the grill didn't have the full smoke-kissed flavor that the visuals promised. In such circumstances, there was only one person to call: Lord Logs, aka Mark Parr, whose company, the London Log Co., does business much as its name suggests. Mark arrived the next day with a truckload of seasoned woods drawn from orchards and forests across southern England. From conversations between Nuno and Mark, a Firehouse blend of aromatic woods came into place: hazel, cherry, oak, and beech, with Japanese charcoal (for its lack of smokiness) as the fire agent. And from there emerged a signature style of cooking, melding the aggressive beauty of fire with a sophisticated knowledge of protein behavior.

"When sous vide came out, it gave chefs a new technique of slow-cooking," says Nuno. "It was a big improvement on the old-school style, of incinerating meats on a gas grill or blasting them in a red-hot frying pan. But in the end, I just couldn't eat red meat from a sous vide. The taste of the blood is plain off-putting. So we started reenacting the process of sous vide in a much more interesting and flavorful environment."

STEAKS—THE FIREHOUSE WAY

The procedure goes like this: the steaks and Iberico pork *presas* are first brought to room temperature, then placed on a high rack above a fire that has flamed out but is still smoking, supplying an optimum heat of 100°F/40°C. The meats are turned and basted every five or so minutes, for a period of 45 minutes to 1 hour.

"The smoke and circulation of the air are the key elements: they're like a hot breeze that slowly brings the meat to its correct internal temperature. They are basically cooked before they're moved over to the hot side of the grill to finish. Because the meat has been cooked at a lower temperature, the pores are open and the meat is relaxed, which is the perfect opportunity for seasoning and a final basting with butter. The smoking has already given us a nice char, so the final few minutes are really about caramelizing the crust. Once again, we keep the meat moving, turning it constantly, so it doesn't get too much heat."

"The smoke and circulation of the air are the key elements: they're like a hot breeze that slowly brings the meat to its correct internal temperature."

The proof of a perfectly cooked piece of meat? The rich flavor profile and the pinkness of the meat extending to the very edge of the crust. Even the faintest band of gray indicates that a steak has been insensitively handled.

AGED BEEF FILET WITH MUSHROOM CARAMEL, ROASTED ONIONS, AND KALE

This dish hits our guests' palates with an umami bomb of meaty and mushroomy goodness, and is a real crowd pleaser. We use aged meat from old Galician dairy cows, which has a deep flavor and works really well with the smoke of our grill. To enhance the meat, we serve it with a mushroom caramel, which originates from one of my first culinary ventures in London, The Loft Project.

INGREDIENTS

Serves 4

FOR THE MUSHROOM CARAMEL:

4½ tablespoons/65 g unsalted butter
9 ounces/250 g cremini or chestnut
  mushrooms, thinly sliced
1 tablespoon honey
1 tablespoon soy sauce
½ cup/125 ml water
½ teaspoon sherry vinegar, or to taste

2 pounds/1 kg 48-day aged beef filet,
  ideally from grass-fed cows, at room
  temperature
Melted butter, for brushing
2 red onions
4 tablespoons sherry vinegar
4 tablespoons water
4 tablespoons superfine sugar

½ large loaf rustic white bread,
  crusts removed
Extra virgin olive oil, for brushing

FOR THE KALE:

2 tablespoons unsalted butter
1 tablespoon freshly squeezed
  lemon juice
1 tablespoon sherry vinegar
Salt
14 ounces/400 g kale, washed, trimmed
  (thicker stalks removed), and coarsely
  chopped

Very good quality extra virgin olive oil,
  for drizzling
Maldon sea salt and freshly ground
  black pepper, to serve

MAKE THE MUSHROOM CARAMEL

Melt 1½ tablespoons of the butter in a saucepan over medium heat, then add the mushrooms in a single layer and cook them for 5 to 10 minutes, until browned and all moisture from the mushrooms has evaporated. Leaving the mushrooms in the pan, add the honey and soy sauce to deglaze the pan. Add the water and simmer until it has reduced by 70 to 80 percent. Transfer the mushroom caramel to the bowl of a food processor or to a blender and blend on high power for 5 to 7 minutes, until smooth.

Make a *beurre noisette* by melting and heating the remaining 3 tablespoons of butter in a hot frying pan until nut-brown and sizzling, then remove from the heat and pour the butter into a heatproof bowl to stop it cooking. Slowly pour the mushroom caramel into the blender (while the motor is running) until the mixture is emulsified. Adjust the seasoning with the sherry vinegar, adding a pinch of salt if necessary.

GRILL THE BEEF

Preheat the oven to 200°F/100°C. Season the meat and put it straight onto a smoking hot barbecue grill or a ridged grill pan. Grill for 20 seconds on each side, to make char marks on both sides. Place the steak on a rack sitting over a shallow roasting pan, brush with a little melted butter, and season with plenty of salt and black pepper.

CONTINUED

Transfer to the oven and cook for 12 to 15 minutes, or until the meat reaches an internal temperature of 110°F/45°C on a probe thermometer, or cook in a frying pan over as low a heat as possible until the meat reaches an internal temperature of 110°F/45°C. Remove from the heat and set aside.

GRILL THE RED ONIONS

Roast the red onions, whole and unpeeled, directly on the dying embers of your barbecue (not on red-hot embers, as they will burn), until dark on the outside and soft inside. Alternatively, roast them (whole and unpeeled) in the oven at 400°F/200°C for 50 to 60 minutes, until soft. Remove (but keep the oven on) and set aside to cool, then peel off the outer layers, cut into quarters, and separate each layer into individual "petals." Combine the sherry vinegar, water, and superfine sugar in a saucepan, place over medium heat and bring to a boil, until the sugar dissolves. Remove from the heat and brush the onion petals with the mixture just before you serve.

MAKE THE CROUTONS

Cut the bread into four ¼-inch/5-mm-thick slices. Brush with olive oil and season with salt and pepper then transfer to a baking sheet and bake for 15 minutes, turning once, until golden brown. Remove and set aside.

COOK THE KALE

Heat the butter, lemon juice, and sherry vinegar in a very big saucepan over low heat. Increase the heat and tilt the pan to swirl the mixture. Once it starts emulsifying, season well with salt and add the kale, letting it wilt, and turning it with a spoon for 3 to 4 minutes, until it is just al dente. Remove from the heat.

SERVE

Gently reheat the mushroom caramel in a saucepan and warm the onions and croutons in the oven. Put the meat back on the grill or grill pan for 30 seconds on each side, to give it a final sear. Brush with butter and season.

Warm 4 plates. Put 2 spoonfuls of mushroom caramel on the warm plates, then slice the steak and place slices on top of the caramel. Top with onion petals, croutons, and kale. Drizzle generously with extra virgin olive oil, sprinkle with Maldon sea salt and black pepper, and serve.

IBÉRICO PORK WITH CHARD MISO AND ZUCCHINI

For some years I have been championing acorn-fed Black Foot Ibérico pork, native to Portugal and Spain. Some guests have heard of it, but it is still news to many just how good the fresh meat is: it has a complex and sweet nutty flavor that is hard to rival. The amazing pigs that we cook at the Firehouse—the same pigs that are used to make the famous Ibérico ham—are raised and cared for by my dear friend Manuel Maldonado and they spend their life eating acorns on the border of Portugal and Spain. They don't care about nationality and they don't have a passport, they just worry about finding the best acorns. The *presa* is the cut from between the top of the shoulder and the beginning of the loin, and is a beautiful, tender cut.

The meat, which you can find online or from a specialty Spanish supplier, needs to be cooked slowly and gently to medium-rare doneness, and should be well rested before serving. I promise you that this will be a revelation!

INGREDIENTS

Serves 4

FOR THE CHARD MISO:

10 ounces/300 g grilled zucchini, finely diced
7 ounces/200 g chard, blanched in heavily salted water, dried, split into stems and leaves, and finely chopped
½ bunch chives, finely snipped
½ bunch mint, leaves finely chopped
2 tablespoons dark miso paste
2 tablespoons toasted black sesame seeds, crushed with ½ teaspoon salt
Juice of ½ lemon
4 tablespoons chive oil (see page 183)
4 tablespoons mint oil (see page 183)

FOR THE ZUCCHINI:

8 baby zucchini, halved lengthwise
Grapeseed oil

A 1¾-pound/800-g whole piece Ibérico pork presa (if you can't find any, very good-quality pastured pork would work, but it won't produce the same excellence as the presa)
If using a charcoal or wood-fired grill: log of wood (birchwood, oak, cherry, or apple)
If using a pan: 1 tablespoon grapeseed oil
8 tablespoons/65 g unsalted butter, melted
Maldon sea salt, to season
Extra virgin olive oil, to serve

MAKE THE MISO

Mix the diced zucchini and chopped chard with the chives and mint in a bowl, then add the miso paste and the crushed black sesame seeds. Mix and adjust the seasoning to taste, then let it sit for 30 to 40 minutes at room temperature in a covered container.

BRINE THE ZUCCHINI

Place the halved zucchini in a 10 percent salt brine (10 percent salt to 100 percent water) for 20 minutes, then drain and pat dry.

CONTINUED

GRILL THE PRESA

Cut the *presa* into 4 equal-sized pieces and let them come to room temperature before you start cooking.

If you have a charcoal or wood-fired grill, smoke the meat slowly over a smoking log for 45 minutes, turning it frequently. Transfer the smoked meat to a hot broiler and cook it for 45 to 60 seconds on each side. Between each side, remove the meat from the heat and let it rest for 5 to 10 minutes. Repeat the broiling and resting process 4 to 5 times until the meat is grilled on all sides and reaches an internal temperature of 118°F/48°C on a probe thermometer. Brush the meat all over with melted butter, including the milk solids, and season with salt.

If you don't have a charcoal or wood-fired grill, heat the grapeseed oil in a heavy-bottomed pan over high heat, swirling it around so that the surface is well-greased. Once the oil is very hot, sear the pieces of meat on all sides, giving each side 45 seconds of direct heat, then removing it to let it rest for 5 minutes, before turning it and searing another side. Repeat the searing and resting process 3 to 4 times until the meat reaches an internal temperature of 118°F/48°C on a probe thermometer and is seared on all sides. The meat will continue to cook off the heat, so stop searing the meat once it reaches 108°F/42°C, then let it slowly reach 118°F/48°C as it rests. Brush the meat all over with melted butter, including the milk solids, and season with salt.

SEAR THE ZUCCHINI & WARM THE MISO

Gently warm the miso in a saucepan (don't cook it!), add the lemon juice, adjust the seasoning to taste, and mix in the chive oil and mint oil.

Heat a little grapeseed oil in a nonstick frying pan and sear the brined zucchini halves, flesh side down, then turn them over and cook them on the skin side. This process should take no more than 3 minutes. Transfer them straight to 4 warm serving plates.

SERVE

Quickly flash-fry the *presa* on both sides in the same pan you used to sear the zucchini, then carve. Arrange 2 to 3 tablespoons of the chard miso in the center of each plate. Place slices of pork neatly on top, then 4 of the seared zucchini. Drizzle with extra virgin olive oil, sprinkle with sea salt, and serve immediately.

CREAMED CORN

Corn is synonymous with summer in North America. I still remember, from my days living in New Mexico, the smell of corn in the husk roasting on a grill. The smoky sweetness of the corn as it's cooked and the husks burn away is the perfect starting point for something special. This lovely recipe is one that our joint head chefs, Patrick and Sebastian, came up with together. During summer in London, we make a point of bringing it onto the Firehouse menu.

INGREDIENTS

Serves 6

FOR THE CORN PURÉE:

3 whole corn cobs
2 tablespoons unsalted butter
1 large leek, thinly sliced
1 large clove garlic, finely chopped

TO FINISH:

3 whole corn cobs
1 tablespoon crème fraîche
1 pickled jalapeño chile
   from a jar, diced
2 teaspoons snipped chives
Juice of 1 lime
Maldon sea salt

MAKE THE CORN PURÉE

Hold the corn cobs upright on a chopping board and cut the kernels off the cobs of corn. Place the kernels in a bowl—you should have about 12 ounces/350 g of kernels. Place the cobs in a large saucepan and cover with 1 quart/1 liter of water, then bring to a simmer and cook for 40 minutes, uncovered, skimming off any scum that rises to the surface.

Once the corn stock is made, remove from the heat and discard the cobs. Heat the butter in a saucepan, add the leek, and sauté for about 3 minutes, then add the garlic. Continue to cook for a few minutes over low heat (you don't want the leeks and garlic to brown), then add the corn kernels. Cook for 2 minutes over medium heat, stirring, then add the stock. Bring to a simmer and cook over low heat, partially covered, for 2 hours. Purée with a stick blender and pass through a fine-mesh sieve into a bowl (you don't need to season it at this point). Set aside.

ROAST THE CORN

Preheat the oven to 325°F/160°C. Roast the three remaining corn cobs in the oven for 40 minutes, turning them occasionally, until the kernels are cooked all the way through. Remove from the oven, leave until cool enough to handle, then cut the kernels off the cobs.

SERVE

Heat the corn purée in a saucepan, then drop in the roasted kernels. Stir in the crème fraîche, pickled jalapeño, and chives, and season to taste with lime juice and salt.

CREAMED SPINACH

Creamed spinach is one of the ultimate steakhouse side dishes, and although I've had my fair share of them, it is very hard to find a good one. I always felt this dish would sit perfectly on the Firehouse menu, and it was one of the original dishes. It is pretty labor-intensive if you are cooking for three hundred, as we often are, but it is much easier to make at home. The recipe is slightly complex, but I promise you it will taste fantastic. Make extra—it will keep well for up to 2 days.

INGREDIENTS

Serves 4

1 pound/450 g fresh spinach leaves
Scant cup/220 ml whole milk
1 bay leaf
2 sprigs thyme
2 small onions, 1 peeled and left whole, the other finely chopped
1 clove

4 tablespoons unsalted butter
2 tablespoons all-purpose flour
4 teaspoons bourbon (we like to use Woodford Reserve)
1 tablespoon Dijon mustard
½ teaspoon Tabasco
Maldon sea salt

PREPARE THE SPINACH

Steam the spinach for 10 minutes, then refresh the leaves in ice-cold water. Squeeze out any excess water with your hands, then leave it to drain on paper towels. Coarsely chop the drained spinach and set aside.

INFUSE THE MILK

Place the milk, bay leaf, thyme sprigs, and the whole onion (pierced with the clove) in a saucepan, bring to a boil, then simmer gently over low heat for 20 minutes. Remove from the heat, strain through a sieve into a heatproof bowl and discard the herbs and spices.

MAKE THE BÉCHAMEL

Melt 4 teaspoons of the butter in a saucepan over medium heat, then add the flour and cook, stirring frequently, for 1 to 2 minutes, to form a sandy-gold (blond) roux. Slowly incorporate the milk, stirring continuously, until it is all incorporated, and whisk until smooth, then cook over low heat for 20 to 30 minutes, until it thickens.

PREPARE THE ONION

Melt the remaining butter in a large, heavy-bottomed saucepan, and sauté the finely chopped onion with some salt for 5 minutes. Deglaze the pan with the bourbon, pouring the measured amount from a container rather than directly from the bottle.

FINISH & SERVE

Increase the heat under the pan with the onion, add the spinach, and fry until any liquid has evaporated, stirring but not letting the spinach brown. Add the béchamel and incorporate well, then add the mustard and Tabasco and stir to combine. Remove from the heat, adjust the seasoning to taste, and serve.

GREEN BEAN SALAD

This salad is inspired by one of my favorite Japanese snacks—wasabi peas. It captures the same flavors, turning them into a healthy and delicious dish.

You will need to stock up on some Japanese pantry ingredients to make the salad, but I can assure you that they are so yummy and addictive that you'll quickly find yourself using them in the rest of your cooking.

INGREDIENTS

Serves 4

FOR THE MUSTARD DRESSING:

1 free-range egg yolk
4 teaspoons Dijon mustard
2 teaspoons wasabi paste
½ cup/125 ml grapeseed oil
¼ teaspoon white soy sauce
  or light soy sauce
1 tablespoon freshly squeezed lime
  juice, or more to taste
Maldon sea salt and freshly ground
  black pepper

1 pound/450 g thin green beans
1 shallot, sliced into rings, to garnish
1 tablespoon furikake seasoning,
  to garnish

Blanch the beans in boiling salted water for about 4 minutes, then drain.

To make the dressing, mix the egg yolk, mustard, and wasabi together in a bowl. Gradually add the oil in a thin stream, whisking constantly (you can make the dressing in a food processor or by hand). Add the soy sauce and lime juice to taste, then season to taste.

Toss the cooled, blanched beans in the dressing. Garnish with the shallot rings and the furikake seasoning.

SWEET POTATO PURÉE

This is a true American classic that has been on our menu since we first opened our doors. I first made it as a "special" at the Coyote Cafe in Santa Fe. Although I shelved it for a while until we opened the Firehouse, I've never forgotten the flavor of the well-seasoned, boozy, and buttery purée.

Sweet potatoes are underused in the UK, but this dish will get anyone addicted to this lovely root. This dish is very easy to make yet impressive enough to serve dinner guests.

INGREDIENTS

Serves 4

1¾ pounds/800 g sweet potatoes
7 tablespoons/100 g unsalted butter
2 teaspoons maple syrup

1 teaspoon salt
2 tablespoons bourbon

Preheat the oven to 350°F/180°C and bake the potatoes whole, in their skins, for 45 to 60 minutes, until soft all the way through. Remove from the oven, and when cool enough to handle, split open the skins and scoop out the flesh into a bowl.

Place the butter in a saucepan over low heat and let it melt, then sizzle until it turns nut brown. Add the cooked potato flesh to the brown butter with the maple syrup and salt.

Put the sweet potato mixture and bourbon into a blender or the bowl of a food processor and blend for 5 minutes.

Pass the mix through a fine-mesh sieve into a clean bowl. Stir well and serve hot. If you are making it ahead of time, let it cool, then cover the surface of the purée with plastic wrap and chill until required.

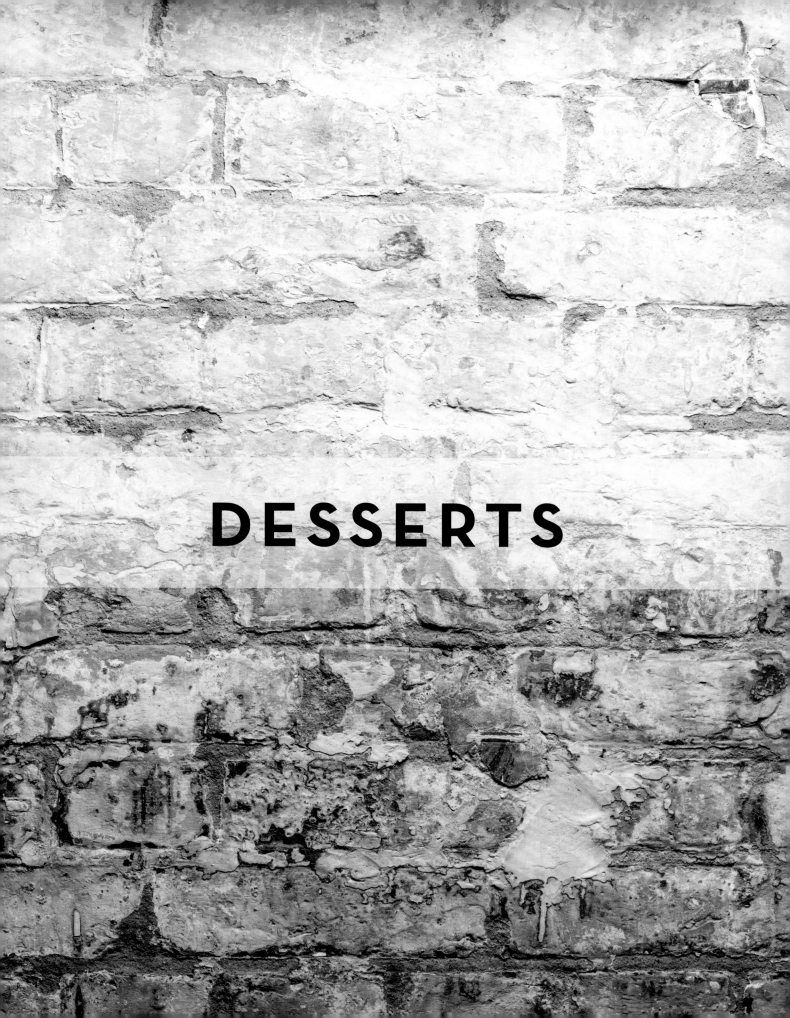

DESSERTS

SUNDAY SUNDAE

One of my favorite childhood desserts was a sundae, and ice cream, whipped cream, and caramel is still a heavenly combination in my opinion. In Portugal, sundaes were usually topped with chopped salted, roasted peanuts, so the addition of something quite savory to the mix was not unusual to me.

Following my travels through Asia, I fell in love with Japanese sour plums (umeboshi). So much so that I started introducing them in paste form to quite a few of my recipes when I was looking for that salty-sour kick. Adding this paste to a fruity caramel elevates it to a perfect balance of sweet and savory and brings back the memories of those childhood Sunday sundaes.

The caramel is an essential part of this dish, but you can experiment with the fruit you add to it, substituting the strawberries for rhubarb, red currants, peaches, or nectarines. If you have some caramel left over, drizzle it over a nice slice of toasted country bread with some clotted cream, or pour it over chocolate mousse. Have fun experimenting!

INGREDIENTS

Serves 4

FOR THE MACERATED STRAWBERRIES:

14 ounces/400 g hulled strawberries, halved
¼ cup/40 g confectioner's sugar

FOR THE CORIANDER CRUMB:

⅔ cup/150 g unsalted butter
⅔ cup packed/120 g soft dark brown sugar
2 tablespoons maple syrup
1 large free-range egg
1⅜ cups/200 g all-purpose flour
⅔ cup/75 g ground almonds
1 teaspoon freshly ground coriander seeds
¼ teaspoon freshly grated nutmeg
¼ teaspoon sea salt

FOR THE STRAWBERRY CARAMEL:

1¾ cups/350 g superfine sugar
9 ounces/250 g hulled strawberries, halved
1 cup/150 g unsalted butter
⅔ cup/150 ml heavy cream
1 vanilla pod, split lengthwise
1⅓ ounces/40 g umeboshi (paste or pitted and coarsely chopped)
Generous pinch Maldon sea salt

FOR THE CHANTILLY CREAM:

1¼ cups/300 ml whipping cream
3 tablespoons confectioner's sugar
Seeds scraped from 1 vanilla pod

4 scoops Milk Ice Cream (page 283), made the day before

CONTINUED

MACERATE THE STRAWBERRIES

A couple of hours before you want to serve the sundae, mix the strawberries and confectioner's sugar in a large bowl. Cover and leave at room temperature to macerate.

MAKE THE CORIANDER CRUMB

Preheat the oven to 350°F/170°C and line a baking sheet with parchment paper. Cream the butter, sugar, and maple syrup together in a bowl for a few minutes. Add the egg and mix well.

In a separate bowl, combine the flour, ground almonds, spices, and salt and mix this into the butter mixture with a wooden spoon until smooth. Tip the dough onto the baking sheet and roll it out into a rectangle around ¼ inch/5 mm thick. Bake for 18 to 20 minutes, until golden brown.

Remove from the oven and allow to cool completely, then break the biscuit into pieces and transfer to a bowl or a strong freezer bag. Using the end of a rolling pin, bash into fine crumbs. Transfer the crumbs to an airtight container until ready to use.

MAKE THE STRAWBERRY CARAMEL

Heat the sugar in a large saucepan over low heat for about 8 minutes, until melted and golden brown (do not stir), watching it carefully to make sure it doesn't burn. Add the strawberries and cook for a few minutes, until they soften. Stir in the remaining ingredients and cook until slightly thickened and it reaches 220°F/105°C on a probe or sugar thermometer. Remove from the heat, take out the vanilla pod, and leave to cool completely.

MAKE THE CHANTILLY CREAM

Whisk together all the ingredients for the Chantilly cream until the cream holds stiff peaks. Cover and chill until needed.

SERVE

Chill 4 bowls. Spoon a dollop of Chantilly cream at the bottom of each bowl. Top with a generous spoonful of macerated strawberries, a drizzle of strawberry caramel, and a sprinkle of coriander crumb. Finally, add a big scoop of milk ice cream and add more caramel and crumbs on top.

SPICED PUMPKIN AND BROWN BUTTER PIE WITH BOURBON CREAM

A good tart is a treat that is really hard to beat. We developed this tart with the goal of merging the spiced pumpkin flavor with the texture of a perfectly soft custard tart. It took a while to get there, but I think we nailed it. This pumpkin and brown butter pie always makes its way into the Firehouse menu on Thanksgiving Day. The pie filling is best made a day in advance, to allow the mixture to settle and any air bubbles to disappear.

NUNO'S TIP
This dish is also amazing served with a scoop of vanilla ice cream, raisins that have been steeped in bourbon and then cooked with brown butter, and finished with a sprinkle of piecrust crumbs.

INGREDIENTS

Serves 8 to 12

FOR THE PUMPKIN PIE FILLING:

½ small pumpkin (about 1 pound/500 g)
3½ tablespoons unsalted butter, diced
2 cups/500 ml heavy cream
4 large free-range egg yolks
1 large free-range egg
3 tablespoons packed soft dark
  brown sugar
1½ tablespoons maple syrup
Pinch Maldon sea salt
1 teaspoon ground cinnamon
1 teaspoon ground ginger

FOR THE SWEET SHORTCRUST PASTRY:

3½ cups/500 g all-purpose flour,
  plus extra to dust
1 cup plus 1 tablespoon/250 g cold
  unsalted butter, diced
2 tablespoons superfine sugar
Pinch Maldon sea salt
2 large free-range egg yolks
⅓ cup/80 ml ice-cold water

FOR THE BOURBON CREAM:

1 cup/250 ml heavy cream
1 tablespoon confectioner's sugar,
  plus extra to dust
3½ tablespoons bourbon

MAKE THE PUMPKIN PIE FILLING

Preheat the oven to 325°F/160°C. Wrap the pumpkin in foil and bake it for 1 hour, then remove from the oven and set aside to cool.

Warm a saucepan over medium heat and drop in the diced butter. Once it melts and begins to foam, whisk it continuously for about 2 minutes, keeping the heat constant, until it becomes nutty and fragrant. The foam will die down a bit, then you will see the color change and the butter solids turn a toasted brown color. Remove from the heat and transfer to a metal jug (it will be very hot) and keep stirring for a further minute to prevent the butter burning (it will keep cooking off the stove).

Peel the baked pumpkin and discard the seeds, then combine 9 ounces/250 g of the flesh in a bowl with the remaining ingredients (including the brown butter). Transfer to a blender and blend until smooth, pass through a fine-mesh sieve into a clean bowl, and skim off any froth on the top. Cover with plastic wrap and transfer to the fridge until you're ready to bake the pie.

MAKE THE SHORTCRUST PASTRY	Place the flour, butter, sugar, and salt in a bowl and mix together, either in a stand mixer fitted with the paddle attachment, in a food processor, or by hand, until the mixture resembles bread crumbs. Add the egg yolks and water and mix until it comes together to form a dough. Wrap the dough in plastic wrap and chill for 1 hour. Preheat the oven to 350°F/170°C.
BAKE THE SHORTCRUST PASTRY	Roll out the chilled pastry on a lightly floured surface to ⅛ inch/2.5 mm thickness, and use it to line a 12-inch/30-cm tart or flan pan. Put the lined pan back in the fridge to chill for 30 minutes to an hour, then prick the surface of the pastry with a fork a few times, line the pastry shell with parchment paper and pie weights and bake for 25 minutes. Remove the tart shell from the oven, remove the parchment and weights, and leave to cool. Reduce the oven temperature to 225°F/110°C.
MAKE THE BOURBON CREAM	Whisk the cream and confectioner's sugar together in a bowl until the mixture forms soft peaks, then fold in the bourbon. Chill until ready to serve.
BAKE THE PIE & SERVE	Pour the chilled filling into the baked tart shell and bake for 1 hour, or until the filling is just set, with a slight wobble. Remove from the oven and let it cool completely before serving with bourbon cream and dusting with confectioner's sugar.

FROZEN APPLE PANNA COTTA

Ooohh… I love this dish! It's one of my favorite desserts and I am so proud of it. It has had several homes: it started life at Bacchus, where we used to make the panna cotta ice cream (which I still love), then it travelled to Viajante, where we added the shiso granita, and finally it made its way to the Firehouse, where we added the burnt meringue, bringing the dish into the world of pavlovas, a very popular dish on North American menus. This dish exemplifies the way I like to cook, and also my belief that dishes should evolve as we evolve.

Make the ice cream, jelly, and granita the day before you want to serve the dessert.

INGREDIENTS

Serves 10

FOR THE APPLE JELLY:

2 sheets gelatin
1 cup/250 ml freshly pressed apple juice
3 tablespoons superfine sugar

FOR THE SHISO GRANITA:

2½ cups/600 ml water
⅔ cup/130 g superfine sugar
2½ tablespoons freshly squeezed
  lemon juice
30 shiso leaves

FOR THE APPLE SPONGE:

1¼ cups/135 g ground almonds
¾ cup/150 g superfine sugar
⅓ cup/50 g freeze-dried apple powder
  (or dried apple pieces blitzed to form
  small crumbs—they will be moister
  than freeze-dried powder, but still
  work well)

5 teaspoons cornstarch
¼ teaspoon salt
3 large free-range eggs
2 large free-range egg yolks

FOR THE ITALIAN MERINGUE:

4 large free-range egg whites,
  at room temperature
2¾ tablespoons water
1¼ cups/250 g superfine sugar
Seeds scraped from 1 vanilla pod,
  split lengthwise

1 Granny Smith apple
Juice of ½ lemon (if preparing
  in advance)
Panna Cotta Ice Cream (page 283)

MAKE THE APPLE JELLY

Soak the gelatin sheets in a small bowl of cold water for 2 minutes, until soft.

Put the apple juice and sugar in a saucepan and bring to a boil. Once the sugar has dissolved, remove the pan from the heat. Squeeze the excess water from the gelatin sheets and stir them into the apple juice mixture until completely dissolved.

Pour the mixture into a Tupperware container, leave it to cool, then transfer to the fridge for at least 2 hours to set.

CONTINUED

MAKE THE SHISO GRANITA

Heat half the water and all the sugar in a small saucepan over medium heat until the sugar has dissolved. Remove from the heat and add the remaining water (to cool the syrup down) and the lemon juice.

Place the shiso leaves in a blender, add the lemon syrup, and blend until it turns into a green juice. Pass the juice through a fine-mesh sieve into a freezer-proof container, to remove any remaining pieces of leaf.

Once completely cool, seal the container and transfer to the freezer. Once the mixture has been in the freezer for 2 to 4 hours, remove it every 25 minutes, scraping the mixture with a fork to break up the ice crystals, until it is fully frozen and flaky (scraping the mixture about 3 times should be sufficient). Keep the granita in the freezer until ready to serve. Alternatively, freeze the granita mixture until solid, then transfer it to the bowl of a food processor and blitz it to break down the ice crystals. Refreeze until ready to serve.

MAKE THE APPLE SPONGE

Preheat the oven to 325°F/160°C and line a baking sheet with parchment paper. Combine the ground almonds, superfine sugar, apple powder, cornstarch, and salt in a mixing bowl. In a separate bowl, whisk the eggs and egg yolks until frothy. Fold the dry mixture into the eggs, ensuring that there are no lumps, until completely incorporated.

Spread the sponge mixture onto the lined tray in an even and flat layer. Bake for 18 minutes, until golden brown. Remove from the oven and carefully transfer the sponge on the parchment to cool on a wire rack.

MAKE THE ITALIAN MERINGUE

Place the egg whites in the bowl of a stand mixer fitted with the whisk attachment.

Put the water, sugar, and vanilla seeds in a small saucepan over medium heat until the syrup reaches 244°F/118°C on a sugar thermometer (begin whisking the egg whites when the sugar mixture reaches 241°F/116°C). When the syrup reaches 244°F/118°C, remove it from the heat and begin to pour it into the egg whites in a steady stream while the whisk is turning, beating the mixture for 8 to 10 minutes, until thick and glossy. You will know when the egg whites are ready as you will be able to hold the bowl upside down above your head without them falling all over you. Transfer the mixture into a piping bag fitted with a small, plain round nozzle and leave in the fridge until ready to serve.

SERVE

Chill 10 bowls. Peel, core, and dice the apple and divide it between the chilled bowls. If you're preparing the dessert in advance, toss the apples in the lemon juice to prevent them discoloring.

Next, break the sponge cake into small pieces and divide the pieces between the bowls. Spoon chunks of jelly among the cake pieces. Don't worry about presentation at this point, as this will all be covered with meringue and granita.

Place a generous scoop of ice cream in the middle of each bowl, and pipe the meringue around it in a circular movement to cover the ice cream completely in a snail shell pattern, curling the meringue in toward the middle.

Toast the meringue with a blowtorch, or put it under a hot broiler for 2 minutes, to make it golden brown, then scatter the granita all around it. Serve quickly before the granita starts to melt.

ENGLISH RASPBERRIES WITH LEMON AND MINT GRANITA

I was once invited to do a demo in New York during the Omnivore Festival. I had travelled from London the day before, and due to strict border controls, I couldn't bring food from our restaurant with me. Instead, I went to Union Square Farmers Market on the morning of the demo and bought the ingredients for this dish. A simple dish, it's all about the quality of the ingredients, and it works perfectly when you want to finish a meal with something light and refreshing. The granita is really lovely in cocktails with vodka and lemon juice, and any leftover mint oil is great with lamb: it will keep chilled for 5 days, or frozen for up to 6 months.

INGREDIENTS

Serves 4

FOR THE SALTED CREAM:

2 cups/500 ml heavy cream
2 pinches Maldon sea salt

FOR THE LEMON & MINT GRANITA:

5 cups/1.2 liters water
1 cup/200 g superfine sugar
1¾ ounces/50 g fresh mint leaves and stalks, plus 20 fresh mint leaves, finely chopped

¾ cup/185 ml freshly squeezed lemon juice

FOR THE MINT OIL:

3½ ounces/100 g picked mint leaves
7 tablespoons/100 ml grapeseed oil

2 (8-ounce/225-g) baskets raspberries, washed and patted dry
7 ounces/200 g sorrel leaves

MAKE THE SALTED CREAM

Mix the cream and salt together, cover, and store in the fridge until needed.

MAKE THE LEMON & MINT GRANITA

Gently heat the water, sugar, and the 1¾ ounces/50 g mint leaves and stalks in a saucepan until the sugar has dissolved. Bring to a boil, remove from the heat, cover with plastic wrap, and infuse at room temperature for 2 to 3 hours (but preferably overnight). Add the lemon juice, then pass the mixture through a fine-mesh sieve into a shallow container. Transfer to the freezer. Once the mixture has been in the freezer for 2 to 4 hours, remove it every 25 minutes, scraping the mixture with a fork to break up the ice crystals, until it is fully frozen and flaky (scraping the mixture about 3 times should be sufficient). Stir in the chopped mint and freeze until ready to serve.

MAKE THE MINT OIL

Blanch the mint leaves in boiling water for 10 to 15 seconds, then plunge them into ice-cold water. Drain and blitz with the oil in a blender. Transfer the mint oil to a saucepan over low heat and gently fry for 5 to 10 minutes, stirring continuously, until you have brown, crispy particles of mint and the oil is fragrant and dark green. Pass through a fine-mesh sieve lined with cheesecloth or muslin into a container, and chill.

SERVE

Chill 4 serving bowls. Scatter half the raspberries in the bowls. Dollop salted cream on top, then granita. Add more raspberries and drizzle with mint oil. Scatter with plenty of sorrel leaves and serve immediately.

LIME PIE

This modern twist on the classic American Key lime pie encases the lime curd in a buttery rye biscuit shell, which the curd oozes out from when cracked open with a spoon. Make the curd a day in advance if you can, so that it's frozen completely solid before you dip it in the biscuit shell. At the restaurant we serve it topped with tiny fragments of lime frozen in liquid nitrogen.

You will need eight 3-inch/8-cm round mousse rings for this recipe.

INGREDIENTS

Makes 8 individual pies

FOR THE LIME MERINGUE:

4 ounces/125 g free-range egg whites
  (about 4 egg whites)
⅜ cup/125 g superfine sugar
⅞ cup/120 g confectioner's sugar, sifted
Grated zest of 1 unwaxed lime,
  plus extra to serve

FOR THE LIME CURD:

¾ cup/150 g superfine sugar
⅟₂₀ ounce/1.5 g agar flakes
3 large free-range eggs

⅔ cup/150 ml freshly squeezed
  lime juice
⅞ cup/200 g cold unsalted butter,
  cubed, plus extra for greasing

FOR THE RYE BISCUIT:

1¼ cups/200 g rye flour
7 tablespoons/100 g unsalted
  butter, diced
½ cup/100 g superfine sugar
1½ cups/300 g cocoa butter, melted

Mascarpone, to serve

MAKE THE LIME MERINGUE

Line 2 baking sheets with parchment paper. Place the egg whites in a spotlessly clean, grease-free bowl and whisk with a hand-held electric whisk or in a stand mixer until light and frothy, then add the superfine sugar a little at a time, until it's all incorporated, continuing to whisk until stiff peaks form. Fold in the confectioner's sugar and spread the meringue mixture over the lined trays until it's about ¼ inch/5 mm thick, then scatter the grated lime zest over the top. Dehydrate in a low oven (100°F to 150°F/40°C to 65°C) until crisp, about 45 minutes, then turn the oven off and leave the meringue to dry overnight. When dry, break the meringue into shards and store in an airtight container until required (the meringue can be made up to 2 days in advance).

MAKE THE LIME CURD

Mix the superfine sugar and agar together in a mixing bowl. Place the eggs and lime juice in a saucepan, add the superfine sugar and agar, and slowly bring to a boil over low heat, whisking continuously to ensure the mixture doesn't catch on the bottom of the pan, until the agar flakes have dissolved. As soon as it reaches boiling point, remove the pan from the heat and add the cold diced butter a piece at a time, emulsifying the mixture with a stick blender. Pass the curd through a fine-mesh sieve into a heatproof container, cover the surface of the curd with a piece of plastic wrap to prevent a skin from forming on top, and leave to cool.

CONTINUED

FREEZE THE LIME CURD

Grease the inside of the mousse rings and line a baking sheet with parchment paper. When the curd is cool, transfer it to a piping bag fitted with a medium nozzle and pipe about ⅓ cup/80 g into each of the greased mousse rings on the lined baking sheet. Place the filled mousse rings in the freezer, then, once the curd is frozen solid (this takes about 3 hours), press each curd out of its mold with a toothpick. Return to the freezer until you are ready to start dipping them.

MAKE THE RYE BISCUIT

Preheat the oven to 325°F/160°C and line a baking sheet with parchment paper. Mix the flour, butter, and sugar together in a bowl to form a crumbly dough, then scatter the dough onto the lined baking sheet. Bake for 25 minutes, until it is firm and golden brown. Remove from the oven and allow to cool slightly, then transfer to the bowl of a food processor or blender and pulse until you have a fine crumb. Add the melted cocoa butter and continue blending to form a smooth liquid batter. Pour the batter into a saucepan and keep it warm (ideally at around 100°F/40°C) by placing it periodically over low heat or a bain marie, whisking it regularly to ensure the mixture stays emulsified.

Line another baking sheet with parchment paper. Remove the lime curds from the freezer and dip them, one by one, into the liquid biscuit coating, making sure they're completely covered. Allow any excess mixture to run off, place them on the lined baking sheet and freeze for 10 minutes, then dip them in the mixture again. Return the coated lime curds to the freezer for 10 minutes to harden, or store in the freezer for longer, if preparing them in advance.

SERVE

Transfer the lime curds to the fridge for at least 1 hour before serving: the biscuit shell will remain hard while the curd will become soft and oozy.

Place a lime pie in the center of each plate, top with a large dollop of mascarpone, shards of lime meringue, and more grated lime zest.

BLOOD ORANGE AND CAMPARI GRANITA, SWEET FENNEL, AND CRÈME FRAÎCHE

I have had many granitas in my life but the one that thrilled me and made me want to make them myself was at Noma in Copenhagen, in 2008. It was served with sweet prawns, dill, and cream. It inspired me to try to capture the essence of amazing fruits and vegetables, such as the orange and fennel in this dish, in cold and crunchy textures.

Blood orange has a short season, so we try to use it as much as we can while it's around. A granita is my favorite way to serve it at the Firehouse.

INGREDIENTS

Serves 4

FOR THE BLOOD ORANGE GRANITA:

5 tablespoons/70 ml Campari
2½ cups/600 ml freshly squeezed blood orange juice
5 tablespoons/60 g superfine sugar
¼ cup/60 ml water

FOR THE CONFIT FENNEL:

1 fennel bulb
¼ cup/50 g superfine sugar
Juice of 1 lemon

⅔ cup/100 g crème fraîche
2 blood oranges, peeled and segmented

MAKE THE BLOOD ORANGE GRANITA

Pour the Campari and blood orange juice into a large container suitable for freezing.

Gently heat the sugar and water in a small saucepan until the sugar has dissolved, then add it to the orange juice and Campari. Place in the freezer and allow to freeze hard (this will take about 3 hours). Once the mixture has been in the freezer for 2 to 4 hours, remove it every 25 minutes, scraping the mixture with a fork to break up the ice crystals, until it is fully frozen and flaky (scraping the mixture about 3 times should be sufficient). Keep in the freezer until needed.

MAKE THE CONFIT FENNEL

Discard the outer layer of the fennel and remove the base of the bulb. Slice the bulb into thin slivers using a mandoline or sharp knife, retaining the fronds for garnish.

Mix the fennel slivers with the superfine sugar in a mixing bowl until the fennel juice starts to come out. Add the lemon juice, cover, and chill until ready to serve. You can make it up to 1 day in advance.

SERVE

Freeze 4 serving bowls ahead of time. Place a dollop of crème fraîche in the bottom of each bowl and top with the sweet fennel and segments of blood orange. Top with the granita and a few fennel fronds.

CHOCOLATE TART

Marco Pierre White wrote in his book *White Heat* about a chocolate dessert that he hated but still served, because the guests wanted it. This is a ballsy statement but something that we mustn't forget in hospitality… No matter how adventurous we are, at the end of the day, we are still here to offer an experience that pleases our guests. They like chocolate and so do I. It can be safe and boring, but when our guests eat it, they always smile. We have changed the garnishes quite a few times, but this tart has been on the menu since we opened and it is still crazily popular. Thanks, Sebastian, for this and many other Firehouse classics.

INGREDIENTS

Serves 8 to 12

FOR THE CHOCOLATE PASTRY:

½ cup/125 g unsalted butter, at room temperature
⅞ cup/125 g confectioner's sugar, sifted
1 teaspoon fine sea salt
1 large free-range egg
1 large free-range egg yolk
1¾ cup/240 g all-purpose flour, sifted, plus extra to dust
½ cup/50 g unsweetened cocoa powder

FOR THE CHOCOLATE CUSTARD FILLING:

9½ ounces/270 g Valrhona Caramelia chocolate or any good-quality chocolate (40 percent cocoa solids), broken into small pieces
8 ounces/230 g Valrhona Andoa dark chocolate or any good-quality chocolate (70 percent cocoa solids), broken into small pieces
¾ cup/200 ml whole milk

1¼ cups/300 ml whipping cream
1 teaspoon salt
3 large free-range eggs

FOR THE CHOCOLATE TWIGS:

5 ounces/150 g Valrhona Andoa dark chocolate, or any good-quality chocolate (70 percent cocoa solids), broken into small pieces
½ cup/50 g unsweetened cocoa powder

FOR THE CHOCOLATE TUILES:

⅔ cup/200 g liquid glucose syrup
7 ounces/200 g white fondant
2 ounces/60 g Valrhona Andoa dark chocolate, or any good-quality chocolate (70 percent cocoa solids), broken into small pieces

Crème fraîche, to serve

MAKE THE PASTRY

Cream the butter, confectioner's sugar, and salt together in a bowl with a hand-held electric whisk or in a stand mixer. Add the egg and egg yolk, beat again to incorporate, then add the flour and cocoa powder. Wrap the dough in plastic wrap and put in the fridge to rest for 1 hour. Once chilled, roll out on a lightly floured work surface to a thickness of ⅛ inch/2.5 mm and use it to line a 7-inch/18-cm round or square tart case. Pop the case back in the fridge for 1 hour before baking, and preheat the oven to 325°F/160°C.

Line the tart shell with parchment paper and cover the base with ceramic pie weights. Blind bake the tart shell for 20 minutes, then remove the parchment and pie weights and return to the oven to bake for a further 5 minutes, or until the pastry base is completely dry. Remove the pastry shell from the oven, set aside, and reduce the oven temperature to 200°F/100°C.

CONTINUED

MAKE THE CHOCOLATE CUSTARD FILLING

Place the chocolate in a large heatproof bowl. Put the milk, cream, and salt in a saucepan and bring just to a boil, then pour onto the chocolate and stir until the chocolate has completely melted. Mix the eggs into the chocolate mixture until smooth, incorporating as little air as possible (don't whisk the mixture).

Pour the hot custard into the blind-baked shell while it's still hot, until it sits just below the pastry rim (leaving a ⅛- to ¼-inch/2.5- to 5-mm gap between the filling and the top of the pastry—be sure not to overfill it). Bake for 45 to 60 minutes, until just set. Remove from the oven and leave the tart to cool down to room temperature, then place in the fridge for at least 2 hours to firm up.

MAKE THE CHOCOLATE TWIGS

Melt the chocolate in a heatproof bowl sitting over a pan of simmering water (make sure the bottom of the bowl isn't touching the water). Transfer the melted chocolate to a piping bag fitted with a fine, plain nozzle. Fill a large bowl with cold water and add a handful of ice cubes. Pipe strands of chocolate into the water—they will curl up and set hard almost instantly. Remove from the water with a slotted spoon and leave to dry on a paper towel. Put the cocoa powder in a sieve and dust it over the chocolate twigs, then put them in a container and keep them in the fridge until needed.

MAKE THE CHOCOLATE TUILES

Line a baking sheet with parchment paper. Melt the glucose and white fondant together in a saucepan over medium-low heat, then let the mixture bubble for 5 to 10 minutes, until it takes on a light caramel color. It may get smoky during this time, but this is fine. Quickly stir in the chocolate until it melts and is fully incorporated, then pour the mixture onto the parchment paper. Leave to cool and harden. Preheat the oven to 350°F/180°C.

Break the hardened mixture into pieces and grind it in a food processor until it forms a fine powder. Using a fine-mesh sieve, sprinkle a thin layer of the powder onto a silicone baking mat or baking sheet lined with parchment paper and bake for 3 to 4 minutes. The mix will melt and form a thin bubbly layer. Remove from the oven and allow to cool. Lift the tuiles off the silicone baking mat or parchment and store in an airtight container until ready to use.

SERVE

Serve a slice of the tart with a dollop of crème fraîche and top with the chocolate tuiles and twigs.

CHILTERN CARROT CAKE

Every once in a while, we have a dish idea that transcends from the savory world into the sweet world.

I have believed for a long time that every ingredient is a complex ingredient, with its natural sugars, natural salts, bitterness, sourness, and fat. All it takes is a change in perspective and ingredients can easily transcend their common place into a new world; the chef just needs to understand how to steer that particular facet of the product into a new light.

This signature dessert started out as a turbot and carrot main course dish. We liked it so much that we turned it into a vegetarian dish, focusing on the carrots. It was very popular, but every time we tasted it, the sweetness of the dish was so interesting that at some point we decided to try it as a dessert. Interestingly, it didn't take too much tweaking to make it into our classic Chiltern Carrot Cake.

INGREDIENTS

Serves 12 to 16

FOR THE HORSERADISH ICE CREAM:

2½ cups/600 ml whole milk
1 cup/250 ml whipping cream
2 ounces/60 g freshly grated
  horseradish
2 sheets gelatin
⅞ cup/175 g superfine sugar
⅓ cup/50 g nonfat dry milk
Pinch Maldon sea salt

FOR THE CAKE:

2 vanilla pods
4 free-range eggs
1⅔ cups/280 g golden superfine sugar
½ cup/125 ml grapeseed oil, plus extra
  for greasing
½ cup/125 ml walnut oil
2 cups/280 g all-purpose flour
1 teaspoon baking soda
2 teaspoons baking powder
1 teaspoon Maldon sea salt
2 teaspoons ground cinnamon
2 ounces/60 g walnuts, coarsely chopped
2 ounces/60 g pecans, coarsely chopped
14 ounces/400 g carrots, grated
¾ ounce/20 g fresh ginger, peeled
  and grated

FOR THE CARROT CARAMEL:

⅞ cup/175 g superfine sugar
½ cup/125 ml carrot juice
5 tablespoons/70 ml heavy cream
1 teaspoon Maldon sea salt
1 vanilla pod, split lengthwise
7 tablespoons/100 g brown butter
  (see technique on page 128)

FOR THE PECAN GRANOLA:

1¼ cups/125 g rolled oats
4 ounces/125 g pecans,
  coarsely chopped
1 tablespoon grapeseed oil
2 tablespoons packed soft light
  brown sugar
2 tablespoons maple syrup
Small pinch Maldon sea salt

FOR THE VANILLA SYRUP:

Seeds scraped from 1 vanilla pod
¾ cup/150 g golden superfine sugar
⅔ cup/150 ml water

4 heritage carrots, to serve
Nasturtium leaves, to serve (optional)

CONTINUED

**MAKE THE HORSERADISH
ICE CREAM**

Make the ice cream the day before you want to serve the carrot cake.

Pour the milk and cream into a bowl and add the grated horseradish. Cover and leave to infuse for 12 hours in the fridge, then pass through a fine-mesh sieve into a large saucepan.

Place the gelatin sheets in a small bowl of cold water and set aside to soak. Add the sugar, dry milk, and salt to the infused milk and cream mixture and place over medium heat. Bring to a boil and cook for 5 minutes, stirring constantly with a silicone spatula, until well incorporated and the sugar has dissolved. Remove from the heat, squeeze excess water from the gelatin and add to the hot cream. Mix well until dissolved. Transfer to a plastic heatproof container and cover the surface of the cream with plastic wrap to stop a skin forming. Leave to cool, then chill for at least 4 hours— ideally overnight—then churn in an ice-cream maker according to the manufacturer's instructions. Alternatively, if you don't have an ice-cream maker, freeze the mixture until hard, then process in a food processor until smooth. Keep frozen until needed.

MAKE THE CAKE

Preheat the oven to 325°F/160°C, grease a 12-inch/30-cm round cake pan and line it with parchment paper.

Scrape out the seeds from the vanilla pods and add them to the eggs and sugar in a mixing bowl. Beat in a stand mixer fitted with the whisk attachment (or with a hand-held electric whisk) until light and fluffy, and doubled in volume. Slowly add the oils to the mixture in a steady stream. Remove the bowl from the stand mixer, if using, and gently fold in the dry ingredients with a spatula, followed by the carrot and ginger. Pour into the prepared pan and bake for 45 to 50 minutes in the center of the oven. To check if it's cooked, push a metal skewer into the middle of the cake—it should come out clean. Remove and leave to cool in the pan slightly before turning out onto a wire rack.

**MAKE THE CARROT
CARAMEL**

Place the sugar in a saucepan with 2 tablespoons of water. Heat gently until the sugar dissolves, then increase the heat and cook the syrup until it starts to turn a deep golden honey color. Add the carrot juice and simmer for 2 minutes. Add the cream, salt, and vanilla pod, and cook until the caramel reaches 230°F/110°C on a sugar thermometer. Remove from the heat, add the cold brown butter, and emulsify with a stick blender. Pass through a fine-mesh sieve. When it reaches room temperature, whisk it in a stand mixer fitted with the paddle attachment or with a hand-held electric whisk until thick and creamy. Store in an airtight container in the fridge until needed.

**MAKE THE PECAN
GRANOLA**

Preheat the oven to 325°F/160°C and line a baking sheet with parchment paper. Combine the ingredients, spread them out on the lined tray, and bake for 35 to 40 minutes, stirring the mixture every 10 minutes.

MAKE THE VANILLA SYRUP

Place the vanilla seeds in a small saucepan with the sugar and water. Heat gently until dissolved, then remove from the heat and allow to cool to room temperature.

SERVE

Using a sharp peeler, peel then shave the heritage carrots into ribbons. Tear the carrot cake into bite-sized pieces, arrange in a bowl with a spoonful of the carrot caramel, and top with a sprinkle of granola. Place a scoop of horseradish ice cream on top and cover with heritage carrot ribbons that have been briefly dipped in the vanilla syrup. If you like a peppery bite, add a few nasturtium leaves.

ICE CREAM

I love ice cream, my kids love ice cream, and most people I know love ice cream. Since the early days of Bacchus, I have been very proud of our tasty and often curiously flavored ice creams. We focus on the flavors, complementing them with a rich reduced milk or intense custardy base. The flavor and texture of the ice creams we make at the Firehouse are quite special. We have a very nice (and expensive!) ice cream machine that delivers great results for the volume of guests we serve, but at the beginning, before the ice cream machine arrived, we made our ice creams fresh and to order with liquid nitrogen. Try it some time!

Make the ice cream the day before you want to serve it.

FENNEL ICE CREAM

INGREDIENTS

Makes 1 quart/1 liter

2½ cups/600 ml whole milk
1 cup/250 ml whipping cream
2 fennel bulbs, outer layers removed, and inner tender layers grated

2 sheets gelatin
⅞ cup/175 g superfine sugar
⅓ cup/50 g dry milk
Pinch Maldon sea salt

Pour the milk and cream into a bowl, add the grated fennel, cover, and leave to infuse for 12 hours in the fridge, then transfer to a blender and blend until smooth. Pass the mixture through a fine-mesh sieve into a large saucepan.

Place the gelatin sheets in a small bowl of cold water and set aside to soak.

Add the sugar, dry milk, and salt to the infused milk and cream mixture and place over medium heat. Bring to a boil and cook for 5 minutes, stirring constantly with a silicone spatula, until well incorporated and the sugar has dissolved. Remove from the heat, squeeze excess water from the gelatin sheets and add them to the hot cream. Mix well until dissolved. Transfer to a plastic heatproof container and place a piece of plastic wrap on the surface of the cream to stop a skin forming. Leave to cool, then freeze for at least 4 hours—ideally overnight. Remove from the freezer and blend in a food processor, then refreeze for at least another 4 hours. Keep frozen until needed.

HAZELNUT ICE CREAM

INGREDIENTS

Makes 1 quart/1 liter

9 ounces/250 g skinless hazelnuts
3½ cups/800 ml whole milk
1¼ cups/300 ml whipping cream
2 sheets gelatin

⅞ cup/175 g superfine sugar
⅓ cup/50 g dry milk
Pinch Maldon sea salt

Preheat the oven to 325°F/160°C. Spread the hazelnuts out on a baking sheet and bake for about 20 minutes, shaking the tray after 10 minutes, then returning it to the oven, until the nuts are golden and fragrant. Remove from the oven and leave to cool.

Pour the milk and cream into a bowl, add the whole roasted nuts, cover, and leave to infuse for 12 hours in the fridge, then transfer to a blender and blend until smooth. Pass the mixture through a fine-mesh sieve into a large saucepan.

Place the gelatin sheets in a small bowl of cold water and set aside to soak.

Add the sugar, dry milk, and salt to the infused milk and cream mixture and place over medium heat. Bring to a boil and cook for 5 minutes, stirring constantly with a silicone spatula, until well incorporated and the sugar has dissolved. Remove from the heat, squeeze excess water from the gelatin sheets and add them to the hot cream. Mix well until dissolved. Transfer to a plastic heatproof container and place a piece of plastic wrap on the surface of the cream to stop a skin forming. Leave to cool, then freeze for at least 4 hours—ideally overnight. Remove from the freezer and process in a food processor, then refreeze for at least another 4 hours. Keep frozen until needed.

MILK ICE CREAM

INGREDIENTS

Makes 1 quart/1 liter

1½ sheets gelatin
2½ cups/600 ml whole milk
1 cup/250 ml whipping cream

⅞ cup/175 g superfine sugar
⅓ cup/50 g dry milk
Pinch Maldon sea salt

Place the gelatin sheets in a small bowl of cold water and set aside to soak.

Put the remaining ingredients in a large saucepan over medium heat. Bring to a boil and cook for 5 minutes, stirring constantly with a silicone spatula, until well incorporated and the sugar has dissolved. Remove from the heat, squeeze excess water from the gelatin sheets and add them to the hot cream. Mix well until dissolved. Transfer to a plastic heatproof container and place a piece of plastic wrap on the surface of the cream to stop a skin forming. Leave to cool, then freeze for at least 4 hours—ideally overnight. Remove from the freezer and blend in a food processor, then refreeze for at least another 4 hours. Keep frozen until needed.

PANNA COTTA ICE CREAM

INGREDIENTS

Makes 5 cups/1.2 liters

4 sheets gelatin
1¾ cups/450 ml freshly pressed
   apple juice
⅔ cup/200 g maple syrup

1 tablespoon superfine sugar
1 teaspoon Maldon sea salt
2 cups/500 ml heavy cream

Place the gelatin sheets in a small bowl of cold water and set aside to soak.

Pour the apple juice into a saucepan over medium heat and add the maple syrup, sugar, and salt. Bring to a boil, then remove from the heat. Squeeze excess water from the gelatin sheets and add them to the juice. Stir until the gelatin has dissolved, then stir in the cream. Transfer to a plastic heatproof container and place a piece of plastic wrap on the surface of the cream to stop a skin forming. Leave to cool, then freeze for at least 4 hours—ideally overnight. Remove from the freezer and blend in a food processor, then refreeze for at least another 4 hours. Keep frozen until needed.

BAKED ST. JUDE

Julie Cheyney makes St. Jude cheese from raw cow's milk at White Wood Dairy in north Hampshire. It is milky and gentle, with a silky texture that is perfect when baked. You can buy it online or in person from the Courtyard Dairy or Neal's Yard Dairy. It can be eaten at a variety of ages—we like to use it when it's had a chance to ripen and has taken on a stronger taste (it melts more easily the longer it has to age, too).

You'll have more chutney than you need, but it's worthwhile making the larger quantity. Store it in sterilized jars and it will keep for months; it's great on toast or in sandwiches.

INGREDIENTS

Serves 2

FOR THE CHUTNEY:

1 small pumpkin (about 2 pounds/
  1 kg)—if pumpkin is not in season,
  use squash
4 russet apples
1¼ cups/200 g golden raisins
1¼ cups/300 ml white wine vinegar
1¾ cups packed/300 g soft dark
  brown sugar
⅓ ounce/10 g freshly grated ginger
2 teaspoons mixed spice
2 teaspoons honey
1 teaspoon Maldon sea salt

FOR THE THYME CRUMB:

5 ounces/150 g sourdough bread
10 sprigs thyme, leaves picked
¼ teaspoon nutmeg, freshly grated
¼ teaspoon ground cinnamon
Pinch Maldon sea salt
1 to 2 tablespoons light olive oil,
  to moisten

1 (3½ ounce/100 g) St. Jude cheese
  or other similar soft cheese (use any
  brie-like cheese; just make sure it fits
  in your oven-proof dish)
Bread, toasted, to serve

MAKE THE CHUTNEY

Peel and core the pumpkin and apples and grate them or cut them into small (¼-inch/5-mm) dice. Place the pumpkin and apple in a large saucepan with the remaining chutney ingredients and cook over a low heat for 1½ to 2 hours, covered, stirring occasionally to stop it sticking to the bottom of the pan, until the liquid has reduced and it has become sticky. Remove from the heat and transfer to sterilized jars, keeping back enough to serve with the cheese.

MAKE THE THYME CRUMB

Preheat the oven to 275°F/140°C (for the cheese). To make the thyme crumb, put the bread, thyme leaves, nutmeg, cinnamon, salt, and oil in the bowl of a food processor and pulse until it forms a fine, moist crumb.

BAKE THE CHEESE

Place the cheese in an ovenproof dish that it fits snugly in. Cover with the thyme crumb and bake for about 25 minutes, until golden. Remove from the oven and leave to cool for a couple of minutes.

SERVE

Place the still-warm cheese on a wooden board and serve with chutney and toast.

BRUNCH

FIREHOUSE MARYS

WHERE DID THE BLOODY MARY BEGIN?
There are reports of its being mixed as far back as
1892, but most records tend to point toward either
bartender Ferdinand Petiot in Paris circa 1920, or
Hollywood star George Jessel in Palm Beach, Florida,
also in the twenties. Either way, the first listed recipe—
a combination of vodka, tomato juice, lemon, and
Angostura bitters—dates back to Lucius Beebe's
The Stork Club Bar Book, published in 1946.

The following Firehouse Bloody Marys try to create a balance between
alcohol, citrus, spice, and savory flavors. We have formulated our own
spice mix, adding subtle notes of fresh basil, English mustard, and
Szechuan peppercorns, among others. It is well worth investing the time
to make it. If you are entertaining, the recipe multiplies easily, and it
stores well in the fridge for several days, or can be frozen for up to
two months.

We have formulated our own spice mix, adding subtle notes of fresh basil,
English mustard, and Szechuan peppercorns.

If you like a thick Bloody Mary, instead of stirring or shaking the drink,
try "rolling" the drink—pouring it back and forth between two glasses or
mixing tins—as the tomato juice becomes thinner when it is shaken
or stirred.

FIREHOUSE SPICE MIX

INGREDIENTS

Makes about 1 cup/250 ml

⅔ cup/150 ml Worcestershire sauce
2 tablespoons green Tabasco
½ green jalapeño
3½ tablespoons fino sherry
5 basil leaves
1 teaspoon freshly grated or jarred
  horseradish

1 teaspoon prepared English mustard
1 teaspoon celery seeds
1 teaspoon whole black peppercorns
1 teaspoon whole pink peppercorns
1 teaspoon whole Szechuan peppercorns
1 teaspoon salt

Place all the ingredients in a blender and blend at high speed for 5 minutes. Allow the mixture to settle, then strain and decant it into a sterilized jar or sealable bags. The spice mix will keep well in the fridge for 3 to 4 days, or in the freezer for up to 2 months.

MARY IN A HURRY

INGREDIENTS

Serves 1

3 slices fresh red chile
1¾ ounces/50 ml vodka
3½ ounces/100 ml fresh tomato juice
⅓ ounce/10 ml Worcestershire sauce
⅛ ounce/4 ml fino sherry
5 drops green Tabasco

⅓ ounce/10 ml freshly squeezed
  lemon juice
Flaked sea salt and freshly ground black
  pepper, to taste
1 slice lemon, to garnish

Place the slices of red chile in a mixing glass and use a muddle stick to gently crush them to extract their juices. Add the remaining ingredients, except the lemon slice, and half-fill the glass with ice cubes. Stir 20 times. Check for seasoning and add salt and pepper to taste. Strain into a tall (highball) glass full of fresh ice. Garnish with the lemon slice and freshly ground black pepper.

NYC CLASSIC

INGREDIENTS

Serves 1

1¾ ounces/50 ml vodka
3½ ounces/100 ml fresh tomato juice
⅔ ounce/20 ml Firehouse Spice Mix
  (see opposite)
½ ounce/15 ml freshly squeezed
  lemon juice

Flaked sea salt and freshly ground
  black pepper, to taste
1 celery stick, to garnish
Thinly pared strips of unwaxed lemon
  peel, to garnish

Place all the ingredients, except the garnishes, in a mixing glass half-filled with ice cubes. Stir 20 times. Check for seasoning and add salt and pepper to taste. Strain into a tall (highball) glass full of fresh ice. Garnish with a peeled strip of celery stick, freshly ground black pepper, and some strips of lemon peel.

LONDON SPICE

INGREDIENTS

Serves 1

Leaves from 10 small sprigs cilantro,
  plus an extra sprig, to garnish
1¾ ounces/50 ml gin
3½ ounces/100 ml fresh tomato juice
⅓ ounce/10 ml Firehouse Spice Mix
  (see opposite)

⅓ ounce/10 ml freshly squeezed
  lemon juice
Freshly ground black pepper, to taste
1 strip unwaxed lemon peel, to garnish

Place the cilantro leaves in a mixing glass and muddle until they wilt and become damp. Add the remaining ingredients, except the garnish, and half-fill the glass with ice cubes. Stir 20 times. Strain into a tall (highball) glass full of fresh ice. Garnish with the cilantro sprig, freshly ground black pepper, and lemon peel.

FRIED EGGS WITH WILD MUSHROOMS, PARMESAN, ARUGULA, AND KALE

This simple dish is all about using the best-quality ingredients, and having them prepped and ready to go. The dish is served in the frying pan, so choose the best pan you have.

INGREDIENTS

Serves 1

1 ounce/30 g kale, washed and trimmed (thick stalks removed)
Olive oil, for frying and drizzling
1 tablespoon unsalted butter
1¾ ounces/50 g Champignons de Paris, small chestnut mushrooms, cremini, or cèpes or morels (if you're feeling fancy), cleaned and sliced or quartered
2 ounces/60 g Paris Black mushrooms, small chestnut mushrooms, cremini, or cèpes or morels (if you're feeling fancy), cleaned and cut into bite-sized pieces

2 medium free-range eggs
¾ ounce/20 g arugula leaves
1⅓ ounces/40 g Parmesan cheese, shaved with a peeler
Maldon sea salt and freshly ground black pepper

Blanch the kale in boiling salted water for 1½ to 2 minutes, then drain and transfer to ice-cold water. Drain again, and pat the leaves dry with paper towels, then coarsely chop and set aside.

Heat 1 teaspoon of olive oil and the butter in a large frying pan. Reserve a handful of mushrooms to garnish, then fry the remaining mushrooms until golden. Season with salt and pepper. Cook for a few more minutes, then add the kale and move the kale and mushrooms to the side of the pan to leave room for the eggs.

Add another teaspoon of olive oil and increase the heat to high. Crack the eggs into the center of the frying pan, reduce the heat to low, cover, and allow the eggs to fry gently for about 2 minutes (the steam generated by covering the pan will help them cook).

In a bowl, dress the arugula with oil and salt and scatter it over the pan. Add the Parmesan shavings and the reserved raw mushrooms. Drizzle with more oil and sprinkle with freshly cracked black pepper. Serve the eggs in the frying pan, or plated.

CRAB AND LOBSTER OMELET

For many years I have been very curious about the cuisine of Japan. When I lived in New York City in the late nineties I spent a fair bit of time around St. Mark's Place, not because of the punk rock scene (although I am a huge fan!), but because there were quite a few cool Japanese restaurants in the area that I really liked. For someone who grew up in Portugal and had not been to Japan, this felt as close as it gets to the real thing. There were yakitori joints, a couple of izakaya, a small sake bar, shochu dens, yakiniku houses, Japanese bakeries, some not-so-remarkable sushi bars, and an okonomiyaki and takoyaki shop. While I knew many other Japanese specialties, okonomiyaki and takoyaki were totally new to me and it quickly became my go-to place when I craved an umami fix. My omelet, which can be served in the pan it's cooked in or transferred to plates, is an ode to these classic Japanese dishes.

INGREDIENTS

Serves 4

FOR THE LA RATTE POTATOES:

4 La Ratte or other fingerling potatoes
  (about 3½ ounces/100 g)
1 clove garlic
1 sprig thyme
1 parsley stalk, leaves stripped
  and retained
1 bay leaf
2 tablespoons sherry vinegar
Pinch table salt

FOR THE OMELET:

10 large free-range eggs
1⅓ ounces/40 g cooked crabmeat,
  pushed through a fine-mesh sieve
1 tablespoon mirin
1 tablespoon shiro dashi

FOR THE TOPPING:

1 tablespoon grapeseed oil
3 red onions, thinly diced
2 yellow peppers, seeded and
  thinly diced
2 green peppers, seeded and
  thinly diced
½ teaspoon turmeric
½ teaspoon cayenne pepper
Pinch salt
8 ounces/240 g cooked white crabmeat
4 ounces/120 g cooked lobster meat
Squeeze lemon juice, to taste

FOR THE MAYONNAISE:

1 free-range egg yolk
2 teaspoons mirin
1 teaspoon rice wine vinegar
½ teaspoon hon dashi
7 tablespoons/100 ml grapeseed oil
1 teaspoon freshly squeezed lemon
  juice, to taste
Pinch Maldon sea salt
½ teaspoon shiro dashi or hon dashi
½ teaspoon sesame oil

TO SERVE:

2 shiso leaves, thinly diced
Leaves from 1 chervil stalk
Parsley leaves

CONTINUED

COOK THE POTATOES

Place the potatoes, garlic, thyme, parsley stalk (retain leaves for garnish), bay leaf, and sherry vinegar in a saucepan, cover with water, and season with salt. Bring to a boil, reduce the heat, and simmer for 20 to 25 minutes until the potatoes are just cooked, then drain. While the potatoes are still hot, peel and cut them into ½-inch/1-cm dice, or as small as you can get them. Set to one side in a bowl covered with plastic wrap, or in a sealed container (do not chill).

MAKE THE OMELET MIX

Whisk together the eggs, crabmeat, mirin, and shiro dashi in a bowl. Set aside until ready to use.

MAKE THE REST OF THE TOPPING

Heat the oil in a frying pan over medium heat, add the onions and peppers, and sauté until softened. Once soft, add the diced potatoes, turmeric, cayenne pepper, and a pinch of salt. Cook for 3 to 4 minutes, then add the white crab and lobster meats and cook for a further 1 to 2 minutes. Add a squeeze of lemon juice, to taste.

MAKE THE MAYONNAISE

Place the egg yolk, mirin, rice wine vinegar, and hon dashi in a bowl and beat together. Still beating vigorously, slowly drizzle in the grapeseed oil to form an emulsion. Season with lemon juice, salt, and the shiro or hon dashi, and add the sesame oil.

COOK & SERVE THE OMELET

Preheat the oven to 300°F/150°C. You need to make the omelets one at a time, so place 4 plates in the oven to keep warm. Heat a 10-inch/25-cm nonstick frying pan (with a removable or ovenproof handle) and pour a generous ladle of the omelet mixture into the pan. Swirl it around to allow the mix to evenly cover the base of the pan. Cook for 1 minute over medium heat, then add a quarter of the crab, lobster, and vegetable mix, spreading it out evenly on top of the omelet. Place in the oven for 2 minutes to allow the egg to cook through, then transfer carefully to a warm plate (unfolded) while you cook the next omelet. While the next omelet is cooking, drizzle mayonnaise over the previous plated omelet in a cross-hatch pattern and sprinkle with picked herbs to garnish.

BEEF AND VEGETABLE HASH, POACHED EGGS, AND JALAPEÑO HOLLANDAISE

Living in North America, I fell in love with beef hash. I remember late nights or early mornings in San Francisco, after work or play, finding a great breakfast place or good all-night joint and ordering beef hash with eggs over easy and hash browns, a guilty pleasure that made me either forget or remember the events of the night before. As years passed and memories faded, I changed the dish into something altogether lighter but still with an amazing taste: perfect for brunch on a cold winter's day. If you prefer a vegetarian version, just leave out the beef.

INGREDIENTS

Serves 4

FOR THE HOLLANDAISE REDUCTION:

4 tablespoons white wine
3 tablespoons white wine vinegar
1 shallot, thinly chopped
Pinch Maldon sea salt
Pinch white peppercorns
1 bay leaf
4 tarragon leaves, removed from the stalk

FOR THE HOLLANDAISE:

½ cup/120 g clarified unsalted butter (see page 185)
4 large free-range egg yolks
2 pinches table salt
Pinch cayenne pepper, plus extra to serve
1 tablespoon freshly squeezed lemon juice
2 tablespoons jalapeño Tabasco

FOR THE HASH:

1 red pepper
1 yellow pepper
2 tablespoons extra virgin olive oil
2 onions, cut into ½-inch/1-cm dice
4 tablespoons Worcestershire sauce
3 tablespoons jalapeño Tabasco
4 large portobello mushrooms, cut into ½-inch/1-cm dice
4 tablespoons vegetable stock
5 sprigs chervil, leaves chopped and stalks retained, plus extra to serve
7 sprigs flat-leaf parsley, leaves chopped and stalks retained
1 beef filet steak (about 7 ounces/ 200 g), cut into ½-inch/1-cm dice
Maldon sea salt, to taste

FOR THE LA RATTE POTATOES:

4 La Ratte or other fingerling potatoes (about 3½ ounces/100 g)
1 clove garlic
1 sprig thyme
1 parsley stalk, leaves stripped and retained
1 bay leaf
2 tablespoons sherry vinegar
Pinch table salt

8 large free-range eggs

CONTINUED

MAKE THE HOLLANDAISE REDUCTION

Place the white wine, white wine vinegar, chopped shallot, salt, peppercorns, and bay leaf in a saucepan and place over low heat. Slowly bring to a boil, then simmer for 5 minutes, until reduced by two-thirds of the original volume. Add the tarragon leaves, stir, and remove from the heat. Pass through a fine-mesh sieve into a heatproof bowl and leave to cool.

MAKE THE HOLLANDAISE

Melt the clarified butter in a small saucepan over very low heat, taking care not to let it bubble. Remove from the heat and set aside. Place the cooled reduction in a heatproof bowl, then add the egg yolks and whisk until you have a creamy mixture. Place the bowl over a pan of simmering water, making sure the bottom of the bowl doesn't touch the water, then slowly drizzle in the cooled, melted butter while whisking continuously, and remove from the heat once all the butter has been incorporated. Add the salt, cayenne pepper, lemon juice, and Tabasco; adjust the quantities to taste. Transfer the hollandaise to a small bowl and place plastic wrap directly onto the surface of the sauce, to prevent a skin from forming on top. Keep the sauce somewhere warm (not in the fridge, as you cannot reheat it before serving).

COOK THE PEPPERS FOR THE HASH

Preheat the oven to 350°F/180°C. Place the whole peppers on a baking sheet and roast them for 20 minutes, turning them halfway through the cooking time. (While the peppers are roasting, you can start cooking the potatoes.)

Once cooked, remove from oven, allow to cool for a few moments, then pull out the stalks with the seeds attached. Gently peel the skin off the flesh while the peppers are still warm and discard. Cut the peeled flesh into ½-inch/1-cm dice and set to one side.

COOK THE POTATOES

Cook the potatoes according to the method on page 300.

COOK THE HASH

Heat a large frying pan over medium heat, add half the olive oil and the onions, and fry for 5 to 6 minutes until soft and golden brown. Add the Worcestershire and Tabasco and cook for a further 1 to 2 minutes, until the sauces have been absorbed by the onions, then add the diced mushrooms, potatoes, and peppers. Add salt to taste, cook for about 3 minutes, until soft, then remove from the heat. Add the vegetable stock to moisten (you may not need it all) and finish with chervil and parsley leaves.

Heat a separate frying pan over high heat, add the remaining oil, and fry the beef cubes with a pinch of salt for about 2 minutes, until cooked through. Remove from the heat.

POACH THE EGGS

Poach the eggs according to the technique on page 137.

SERVE

Warm 4 plates (or you can serve the hash in the pan it has cooked in). Add the beef to the vegetable hash and top with 2 poached eggs per person and a generous dollop of hollandaise with an extra pinch of cayenne pepper and some chopped chervil. Serve immediately.

SOFT SCRAMBLED EGGS WITH LEEK, ZUCCHINI, SPINACH, AND PARMESAN

I love breakfast and still believe that it is one of the most overlooked mealtimes of the day. Because we're all rushing around in the morning, we always forget to make this an exciting meal. Since we've had children we have been constantly making an effort to make the morning a special time of day, when we all sit together around the table and enjoy some nice family time. It's funny that this particular dish was something I used to cook at home for my children and my partner, Clarise, in the mornings. I liked it so much that I decided to bring it to the Firehouse and include it on our breakfast menu. I guess this is the biggest test for a chef: if you can impress two two-year-olds and a four-year-old, you can probably put that dish on your menu and leave it there for a while!

It's a winner!

INGREDIENTS

Serves 2

6 free-range eggs
2 tablespoons extra virgin olive oil
½ leek, trimmed, halved lengthwise and thinly sliced
½ zucchini, halved lengthwise and thinly sliced

Handful baby spinach leaves, plus extra to garnish
Grated zest of ½ unwaxed lemon
3 tablespoons finely grated Parmesan cheese, plus fine shavings to garnish
Maldon sea salt and freshly ground black pepper

Break the eggs into a mixing bowl and whisk gently (you don't want them to be fully blended—it's nice to still see some yolk and white unmixed). Set aside until ready to cook.

Heat the olive oil in a frying pan over medium-low heat, add the leek and zucchini, and sauté for about 1 minute until soft. Add the whisked eggs, baby spinach, lemon zest, and grated Parmesan, and salt and black pepper to taste.

Cook over very low heat, stirring gently with a wooden spatula to make sure the egg does not stick to the pan. Cook until you are happy with the consistency—we like to serve them pretty soft at the Firehouse.

Serve immediately, topped with freshly shaved Parmesan and fresh spinach leaves, and some toast if you want.

SMOKED SALMON WITH CORNBREAD PANCAKES AND POACHED EGGS

Smoked salmon is one of my favorite proteins to eat for breakfast. When Ole Hansen, proprietor at Hansen & Lydersen smoked salmon, dropped by my old restaurant Viajante late one night, slightly tipsy from a night of drinking, I was struck by his enthusiasm and passion for his craft. The next morning, a much more composed Ole showed up in his wellies, wearing a yellow raincoat and carrying a beautiful side of smoked salmon. He asked me to try it. I brought out a cutting board, carved it, tasted it, and shared it with the rest of the team. I was so impressed by his product that Hansen & Lydersen Salmon has featured on my menus ever since that first tasting, in the Corner Room and then at the Firehouse. Sadly Ole and I don't speak as often as we used to—our lives are too busy and a coffee with friends has become a luxury that we've given up pursuing—but I still view him as a dear friend. This great dish uses his lovely salmon and it's my way of staying in touch with Ole.

INGREDIENTS

Serves 4

FOR THE CORNBREAD PANCAKES:

⅞ cup/200 g unsalted butter
1⅜ cups/200 g all-purpose flour, sifted
¼ cup/50 g superfine sugar
1 teaspoon salt
½ teaspoon cayenne pepper
2 teaspoons baking powder
3 large free-range eggs
2 tablespoons maple syrup
1 tablespoon truffle paste
¾ cup/120 g frozen corn
5 chives, finely snipped
Leaves from 2 sprigs tarragon

8 slices good-quality smoked salmon (about 3 ounces/80 g per person; we use Hansen & Lydersen)
8 free-range eggs, poached (see page 137)
Maldon sea salt and freshly ground black pepper
4 sprigs chervil, to garnish

Melt the butter in a saucepan over low heat, then remove from the heat and set aside. Mix the flour, sugar, salt, cayenne pepper, and baking powder in a large bowl.

In a separate bowl, whisk together the eggs, maple syrup, and truffle paste. Pour the egg mixture into the dry ingredients and fold everything together. Blend the frozen corn in a blender or a food processor until it forms medium-fine crumbs, then stir them into the egg and flour mix. Fold the melted butter into the mixture, a little at a time so it doesn't split. Fold in the chives and tarragon, cover, and transfer to the fridge to rest for about 4 hours.

When you are ready to cook the cornbread pancakes, place a small nonstick frying pan (ours is 6 inches/15 cm) over medium heat, pour in a mug or ladle of the batter, and fry for 2 minutes on each side, until golden brown. Transfer to a plate and keep warm in a low oven while you make the remaining pancakes and poach the eggs.

Place a pancake on a serving plate and add 2 slices of smoked salmon. Put 2 poached eggs on top. Repeat with the remaining servings. Season to taste and garnish with chervil.

TRUFFLED EGGS

The partnership of truffles and eggs has a long history. At the right time of year, when truffles are at their peak (between October and January/early February, then during the summer months), few things beat very soft scrambled eggs garnished with these pungent gems.

There's nowhere to hide in this basic recipe, so good technique and the highest quality of ingredients are crucial. Free-range organic eggs are a must: you need to use the freshest eggs with the yellowest yolks and richest flavor, and if you follow these steps, I can assure you that this recipe will become a classic worth revisiting every year during truffle season. If you feel so inclined, try the dish with a beautiful white truffle.

INGREDIENTS

Serves 4

8 large, very fresh free-range eggs
Maldon sea salt, to season
4 teaspoons unsalted butter, plus extra
 for spreading
4 teaspoons crème fraîche
4 teaspoons very good-quality
 store-bought black truffle paste

1 small fresh black truffle (about
 2 ounces/60 g), very finely grated
8 tablespoons/6 g finely grated
 good-quality Parmesan cheese
4 teaspoons finely snipped chives
Extra virgin olive oil, for drizzling
2 sprigs chervil (optional)
4 slices country-style bread,
 toasted, to serve

Whisk the eggs thoroughly in a bowl and season with salt.

Melt the butter in a small, shallow heavy-bottomed pan over low heat and swirl it gently around the pan (you don't want it to brown).

Add the whisked eggs to the pan and, using a plastic spatula, continuously and gently stir the eggs so that they don't cook too quickly, for 2 minutes. The eggs should be very wet and loosely scrambled. Once the eggs start thickening and you see small solids forming, remove the pan from the heat and stir in all the remaining ingredients, except the olive oil, chervil, and bread (and retaining some of the grated truffle to garnish), until thoroughly amalgamated.

Transfer the truffled eggs to hot bowls, top with chervil, if using, and the remaining grated truffle, to taste. Drizzle with olive oil and serve immediately with toasted country bread spread with unsalted butter.

Luis Simoes, our head barman and mixologist, spent months developing the recipes for our bottled cocktails. They are the Firehouse Classics, five interpretations of the traditional cocktail, all with a unique recipe, cooked in a sous vide for twenty-four hours. The long heating allows the flavors to round and mellow for a blend of subtle layers. Some think that the flavor profile is even better than that of fresh cocktails—something to be savored after hours.

INDEX

Originally published in slightly different form in Great Britain by
Preface, an imprint of Penguin Random House UK, London, in 2016.

All images copyright Peden + Munk except the devil illustrations,
copyright © Chiltern Street Hotel Ltd.; images on pages 145, 169,
227, 305, copyright © CW Mosier; endpapers, copyright © London
Metropolitan Archives, City of London.

Library of Congress Cataloging-in-Publication Data is on file
with the publisher.

Hardcover ISBN: 978-1-60774-992-9
eBook ISBN: 978-1-60774-993-6

Printed in China

Photographers: Peden + Munk
Editor: James Truman
Design: HERE Design
Recipe tester: Kat Mead
Copyeditor: Laura Nickolls

10 9 8 7 6 5 4 3 2 1

First American Edition

SECTION · C - C

SECTION ·